# Out of The Storm

Chaplain Sy Alli

# Dedication

This book is dedicated to my family: Daughters Tasha Nycole Alli and Samaria Hope Alli. Son Sy Alli the 4th, Granddaughter Joiee Wray Kenney, Sister Rhonda Elaine Alli, and brother-in-law Rick James, aka "Pretty Ricky what they call him." Thanks for always loving me even when I didn't love myself. To my parents, the late Salli Alli Jr. and Joan Ann Alli, may they both rest in peace. Thank you to all those veterans at the Veterans Transition Center in Marina, CA, for accepting me as your brother and chaplain!

# Acknowledgment

I want to thank God first and foremost. Then, my beautiful angel in heaven, my aunt/godmother, Hessina Dolvin Alli, for making my dream project a reality. My Church Family, which includes His Grace Ministries International of Salinas, California (Pastors Enrique and Ileana Cardenas) and Community and Family Builders of Pittsburgh, PA (Ms. Diane Powell), for giving me access to Penn Hills (PA) High School Students. Elevo Learning of San Diego, CA, for my career resurgence as a Youth Coach in Monterey County, CA, and subsequent promotion to Site Success Manager for several school districts on the Central Coast of California. A special acknowledgment to Matt Brown, who was the General Manager of Anytime Fitness in Marina, California, and Sean Hastings, who was the Assistant Manager.

These guys truly opened up the door to the fitness facility when I was a homeless chaplain and living in a veteran's shelter across the street. They gave me huge military discounts and a couple of free months to offset my lack of funds at the time. That was truly needed and appreciated!

# About The Author

Chaplain Sy Alli resides in Carmel, California, where he is a Site Success Manager with Elevo Learning. Chaplain Sy also ministers to several Personal Care Homes in Monterey and works with At-Risk Youths. He has a degree in criminal justice, as well as in religious studies and chaplaincy. He is a father to three adult kids: Tasha Nycole, Samaria Hope, and Sy Alli the 4th. He also has one granddaughter, Joiee Wray Kenney. Being a Suicide Attempt Survivor and having battled with life-threatening PTSD, this book is for all those "Lost Souls" who are out at sea and battling their situations with Depression and PTSD.

Sy has led many lives: USAF European Powerlifting Champ, Actor, Professional Wrestler, University Lecturer, and Dignitary Protection Specialist. His story is of interest to all, as Mental Health has been thrust to the forefront of our society!

# Preface

I was moved to write this book after I became sober on March 1st, 2020, and soon after gave my life to Jesus Christ. After that, I had a complete self-assessment and came to realize that I suffered from massive depression, and had been since the death of my "Two Fathers" and my divorce after 20 years of marriage. I operated in two different worlds, one where I thrived professionally but suffered in complete darkness. God finally came for me, and I'm alive because of him.

# Contents


Dedication ................................................................. i

Acknowledgment ..................................................... ii

About The Author..................................................... iii

Preface ................................................................... iv

Chapter 1: The Beginning ......................................... 1

Chapter 2: "Youngblood" My Pro Wrestling Days............... 12

Chapter 3: Hollywood On The Monongahela................... 16

Chapter 4: Losing Part Of My Soul.............................. 31

Chapter 5: Fatherhood ............................................. 36

Chapter 6: Farewell My Friend ................................... 45

Chapter 7: Strike Two .............................................. 54

Chapter 8: New Beginnings ....................................... 62

Chapter 9: Mental Health Crisis ................................. 69

Chapter 10: Reinvention .......................................... 76

Chapter 11: Olympics (2016)..................................... 84

Chapter 12: The Fresh Prince Of Puyallup..................... 92

Chapter 13: Bliss In Patience .................................... 100

Chapter 14: Faith And Friendship................................ 116

Chapter 15: Pitt Stop .............................................. 126

Chapter 16: California Dreaming ................................. 135

Chapter 17: Coach Sy .............................................. 144

# Chapter 1: The Beginning

Life is like an adventurous roller coaster ride with its adequate share of ups and downs, happiness and sorrows, success and failures. You never know what the next moment might bring for you. One moment, you could be enjoying life, and your entire world could change and fall apart within the blink of an eye. This world is a temporary place; we are all travelers here, living our journey and headed toward what has been destined for all of us. My journey in life has been very courageous and unpredictable at the same time. I have been through some of the best and a few of the worst times, but I held onto it with faith in GOD and never lost hope, even when everything seemed to be falling apart. The day you become hopeless is the day your soul dies; you may be breathing on the outside, but internally, you won't feel anything.

Life has taught me how to be thankful and grateful for our blessings because once we lose them, only then do we realize their importance. So, never waste your time in anger, regrets, worries, and keeping grudges against each other because life is too short to be unhappy. Sometimes, we as humans tend to take life for granted without acknowledging that it is a blessing. We don't realize that if given a chance, people resting in graves today would give anything to return one more time and relive their journey.

Sustaining mental stability is one of life's greatest blessings that improves an individual's general well-being. It promotes emotional equilibrium and clarity while offering resilience in life's obstacles. Effective communication, better relationships, and constructive problem-solving are all made possible by stable mental health, and I am saying all of this through my personal experience. It helps people to pursue objectives with motivation and focus, which promotes success in both the personal and professional spheres. Additionally, mental stability supports physical health because the mind-body connection greatly influences overall vitality.

Improved immune function, less stress, and deeper sleep are all facilitated by a stable mental state. It increases one's ability to be joyful, appreciative, and resilient in the face of difficulty. Consistent mental well-being fosters empathy, comprehension, and communal harmony, which benefits the person and the community. It basically acts as the cornerstone of a contented and meaningful life, empowering individuals to effectively and gracefully navigate life's obstacles.

I have been through a lot of struggles in my life, and there came a point when I felt like giving up and taking my life. I distinctly remember that in a dark and weak moment of my life, I decided to commit suicide and end my life and all the miseries I was going through. It was April 18th, 2015, when I put my Glock 19 in my mouth with the intent of killing myself. However, a voice in me reminded me that I was not a coward and I was better than this, so I stopped and pulled out the gun from my mouth.

I had painstakingly planned the day of my suicide, and even though it was a Saturday, I often went to work. My position was the Director of Corporate Security, which entailed a lot of work with the security systems, security plans, and procedures for a Cannabis company. When I was certain that all the employees had left for the day, I made sure that the facility was completely secure. After that, I retrieved a bottle of Vodka with the plan of drinking a half gallon before I pulled the trigger. However, I was overpowered with courage, and I thought I did not need alcohol to do this.

As I adjusted my office chair, I moved the photo frame placed on the shelf that had a picture of my kids to ensure it would not be splattered with my blood. I did not want the beautiful faces of Tasha Nycole, Samaria Hope, and Sy the 4th to be spoiled with their father's blood. Thus, I readjusted the pictures and proceeded with my ill-advised plan. I turned on the music in my office that day, and I listened to my favorite band, London's own Incognito, an acid jazz band that I had seen live many times. I had a big screen in my office with all the CCTV cameras, so my office was always lit up. I sat in my chair, pulled my Glock 19 out of its holster, and jacked a round in the chamber. I fidgeted a few times and thought that I did not want to feel the pain, so in order to end my misery in a quick and painless manner, I decided to put the pistol in my mouth.

When I finally got into a comfortable position, I was ready to pull the trigger and take my life once and for all. But, the moment I decided to put pressure on the trigger to end my life, my entire office went dark. All the lights, cameras, and music were gone in the blink of an eye, and suddenly, it became dark and completely silent. For a minute there, I thought I was dead already, and my death was absolutely painless; however, there was no brilliant light, which I thought I would experience. There was just pin-drop silence, and that was when things got interesting. I could actually process my thoughts, so I was confused as to what or where I was. I could differentiate if I was alive or dead. I felt an odd sensation as if an electrical charge was going through my body, and then I began to feel the presence of certain individuals around me. I pondered to myself, was this Heaven, or was this Hell?? I dared to guess, but I could not.

As I began to formulate my thoughts, I was downright terrified to decipher what was happening to me. The two individuals who were with me began to move closer, and I could faintly hear them talking. At that moment, I could smell the aroma of those individuals and their presence in my personal space. The scent was that of my father's, Salli Alli Jr., and my father-in-law's, the Rev. Samuel George. Both of them passed away in 2005 and 2009 respectively. I began asking myself questions like, why are they here? Where am I? My heart began to pound faster, which only added to my confusion as I could not understand if I still had life inside of me or not.

My father was crouched on my left side while I could feel the grip of my father-in-law's hand on my right shoulder. I distinctly remembered that grip from our handshakes that we used to have. While I was busy thinking about what was happening, they began to talk, and this time, I could hear them loud and clear. My father was really upset and reprimanded me for being foolish for leaving all my loved ones behind and choosing to end my life, but even then, he did not curse or abuse me. I thought that is what Heaven must do to a person. And then my father-in-law said something to me that I will never forget, he said,

"Son, do you know what you are going to leave behind in your wake?" Before I could answer him, a drop-down projector appeared in front of me, and it flashed my entire life in front of me, beginning from my birth to my actual suicide. It was as if a film was being played in front of my eyes, and the worst part of the whole reel was the climax. When I watched the bit where I shot myself and bled out in my office, the scenes that appeared afterward terrified me to my core. I saw my fellow employees finally entering my office to find my lifeless body and panicking.

The movie then went on to show me how my family was notified and the sadness and anger that my family and friends went through upon hearing the dreadful news of my death. That was the hardest part to watch since there was no turning away or closing my eyes. I looked at my kids, being devastated at the fact that I would take my own life. My kids needed counseling as they looked completely shattered. They also needed guidance for alcohol and drug addiction, which was the outcome of their dad taking his own life. At some point, I peed my pants, and I'm not sure if that was the result of shock or what.

As soon as the movie ended, both of my dads said in unison,

"Is this what you really want?"

By that time, I was a complete wreck, and I still did not know what was happening, but I vividly remember I did whisper, "No" at that moment. Then, the lights came back on my CCTV cameras, all of them slowly illuminated one by one, and the music played once again. The song by Incognito was entitled "Out of The Storm," and it was playing on a loop. I was stuck to my chair as I could not dare to move because of the shock I was in. I could not comprehend what had just happened, and it took me a little while to differentiate between what was real and what was not.

I was soaked with sweat and urine, and I was stunned as I looked at the watch. I could not fathom how incredibly the time had elapsed. I have a vivid recollection that when I sat in my chair to commit suicide, it was 4:00 pm in the evening. However, it was 9:00 pm when I came back to my senses and realized I was still alive. I asked myself, what the heck just happened?? And I thought maybe someone played a trick on me or something. At the same time, I thought that I was neither drunk nor I was high on any sort of drugs, so I was definitely not tripping. I carried all of this in the back of my soul for five years until I came full circle!

I believe it takes a lot to get to a point where you no longer have the desire to live, and I reached that threshold after being through countless hardships. I guess the bitter experiences of my life took a toll on my mental health in some way, but I did not realize it initially, and I only came to know about it when it took the best of me. It was 1979 when I decided to join the United States Air Force (USAF), and I had just graduated from high school. I vividly remember that I attended USAF Basic Training in September of 1979, and after that, I stayed in San Antonio (Lackland AFB) on account of my Law Enforcement/ Security Police and Air Base Ground Defense Training at Camp Bullis, which was right outside of San Antonio.

When I was done with my training, I was sent to the Bitburg Air Base located in West Germany (the name it was known by at that time). Truth be told, I was a young man full of life who was let loose in a place like Europe, and I had the time of my life! Initially, I was an SP, better known as Security Police, and was responsible for protecting Flightline and all the designated Aircraft areas and Munitions Storage areas. Since I had just graduated from high school, I was quite young and also naïve then. Considering my innocence, I vividly recall buying my first vehicle, a BMW 1800. My supervisor, Staff Sergeant John Jefferson, and his wife, Eleanor (if I remember correctly), sat me down one day and handed over a box of condoms to me. At first, it made me feel a bit awkward; however, as the conversation unfolded, I began to understand the context and enjoy it. I clearly remember he said,

"Sy, you are about to embark on this journey across Europe and Europe, especially German women who love black men. Son, you need to be protected as they would love to have your baby and go to the USA on that basis."

Even though it was a serious conversation and none of them were kidding, I could not control my laughter, so I kept laughing like a maniac while they explained everything to me. However, later on, when I began to roam around Europe and discover new places, I realized that they were correct. I realized what they were talking about when I started going to nightclubs. I had a blast in Europe, and I almost married a Danish woman named Annette. I met her while I was deployed in Aalborg, Denmark.

Annette was absolutely stunning, and I had met her at a nightclub in Aalborg. I fervently remember that all of my fellow Security Police officers tried to get with her the night I met her, but she swatted them all down. I vividly remember the moment she entered the club, as we had made eye contact there, but I still played hard to get her as I knew she was in demand. Eventually, after a while, I went over to her and asked her out for a dance, and then we danced for the remaining part of the night. She had a very athletic build and the most brilliant and catchy blue eyes I had ever seen before. When I returned to Bitburg, she even came down to see me once. I remember I had gotten three days off then and was taking training on those days. I was in the middle of a training class when I received a call from the main gate, and the guy on the other end told me that there was a beautiful woman at the gate asking for "Sy." I instantly knew it would be none other than Annette, so I ran like a fanatic and nearly broke my neck to get to the main gate to see her! I just could not contain my excitement when I laid my eyes on her that day! We hung out together for the entire weekend and had a lot of fun. And when the weekend was over, I took her to the train station myself to drop her off and bid farewell.

Annette was fervent that she wanted to marry me, but I was immature at that time, so I was not ready to make a commitment like marriage. I was still a bit confused, so I sent a picture of her to my dad and told him that she wanted the two of us to get married. My dad adamantly suggested that it was a bit too early for me to get into something like this and that I could not keep up with it. He was absolutely correct about that, but one thing that my dad and I both agreed on was that she was breathtakingly stunning!

The chapter of Annette in my life was closed after a little while, but she was definitely one memorable woman! I remember making several great friendships in the Air Force and seeing a lot of the world.

Eventually, I married a very young woman, a Panamanian/American woman whose family also resided in Bitburg. I married her in Minot, North Dakota, in 1982 and vividly remember how my dad opposed it and told me that I was too immature to handle such a relationship. However, I did not pay attention to it, so I still went ahead with my decision and married her. But I believe my dad was correct, as our marriage lasted for only four years, and we divorced in 1986. That is when I recalled my dad's words when he said I was "too young and dumb" to get married, but I did not listen to him. I was stubborn and thought I knew everything better than my father, but I guess I did not know anything after all, and this bitter experience indicated that. The best thing about Vielka and my union was our beautiful daughter, Tasha Nycole.

While I was stationed at Bitburg Air Base, Germany, I was selected to train with Germany's Elite Counter-Terrorism Unit GSG-9. Only two other people in my unit went to this training, and it was an awesome experience to train alongside the elite counter-terrorism personnel.

That drill aimed to prepare me for my protection career that would take shape in the years to come! I also coached the Men and Women's Powerlifting Team at Hahn Air Base in Germany from 1983-1986. We traveled all across Europe via planes and buses, and I drove the team in a 26-seater passenger bus. Those were definitely fun times, and I enjoyed a lot on every tour.

Throughout my career in the Air Force, I was stationed at multiple locations, including Minot, North Dakota; McGuire AFB, NJ; Andrews AFB, Maryland; Bolling AFB in Washington DC, and Germany, where I was posted twice. I left the Force in 1986 to become a professional Wrestler. If not for that, I would have stayed there for another 20 years.

I returned to the Air National Guard in 1999 in New Jersey. I was later stationed at Andrews AFB for three years, from 20002003, and everything changed after 9/11/2001. There were drastic changes made after the 9/11 incident, and I did not want to be deployed overseas because I had a young family. So, I decide to opt out of serving in the Military.

I lost a really big position with The World Bank due to my activation after 9/11, and I was severely disappointed that I was put on orders, but I would do it all over again. I would like to give a special shoutout to the 13th Security Forces Squadron at Andrews AFB for showing me so much love, as it was a really tough time for me. I will never forget those brothers and sisters who rallied around me, as they were well aware of how much money I lost during that time period. Go, Air Force! I served for seven years in the Military and will cherish all those moments and memories for the rest of my life!

# Chapter 2: "Youngblood" My Pro Wrestling Days

As an Air Force Powerlifter, I had to increase my body weight from 148 pounds to 190 pounds to meet the requirements—all rock-hard muscle. Initially, I used to be lean, so I began throwing around some weights to gain mass. I vividly remember that at the pinnacle of my powerlifting days, I did multiple cardio exercises. I squatted 600 pounds., bench pressed 400 pounds, and I felt like a human deadlifting machine close to 700 pounds. At that point, I could grasp the attention of some of the professional wrestlers while I was at Denver's old Stapleton Airport in 1986.

I have a clear memory of the time I was returning to Germany, and I ran into a few WWF wrestlers at a bar at the airport; I met Tony Atlas and the Iron Sheik along with Ricky Steamboat. I went up to greet them, and somehow, we started a conversation about lifting weights. That was the moment my passion for professional wrestling roused, and I realized how much I adored it. Tony Atlas was the one who asked me if I was athletic or not, which I certainly was.

I had been serving in the Air Force for seven years when I met them, and truth be told, even the thought of becoming a pro wrestler was intriguing but far-fetched to me. I was uncertain if I would make a career out of the United States Air Force. I was quite young, already married to my first wife, Vielka, and had my daughter, Tasha Nycole. So, I truly needed to think things through. In case I change my mind, Tony Atlas gave me the name of a professional wrestling training center located in Milford,

Connecticut. Former Pro Wrestler Tony Altomare, who was one half of the tag team known as "The Sicilians" with Lou Albano, was the lead trainer there. Suddenly, I had a strong urge to pursue a career in wrestling, so I reached out to Tony Altomare, and he explained that if I wanted to be a professional wrestler, I had to stand out from the crowd.

All of a sudden, I began to think quite seriously about leaving the Air Force and making my way into the wacky world of professional wrestling. As I mentioned earlier, I was still quite young and immature to be a husband and a father to a two-yearold kid; however, I decided to give my passion a shot. A voice inside me kept telling me that it was worth giving a try. But what I had not anticipated was the cost I would have to bear, and it turned out to be my marriage to Vielka. I left the Air Force in 1986 and then moved to Milford, Connecticut, to stay at the "Wrestlers Retreat in Milford" with the other wrestlers who, like me, had aspirations of becoming a pro wrestler. My marriage was affected because of this, and as a result, Vielka and I got divorced officially in 1987.

Soon after that, I moved to Pittsburgh in the next few years and joined Tri-State Wrestling as "Sy Youngblood," where I was showing off my acrobatic abilities as an African/ Indian Native American. At first, I had financial difficulties, so I balanced out the finances by driving a Yellow Cab on the side along with wrestling so that I could keep the money flowing in. I often regret that I made decisions based on my immaturity because I had to stay apart from Tasha Nycole, and I missed her. However, I made sure she maintained her relationship with her paternal family by taking her to Pittsburgh on visits despite the many difficulties. As

I began to develop a following in pro wrestling, I embraced a variety of roles and enjoyed entertaining large audiences. Whether there were just 25 or 10,000 spectators, it did not matter to me; I gave each and every performance my all. I was known for being very daring with aerial maneuvers, and this enthusiasm also caused me to leave the professional wrestling scene early. I was living a fantasy life as I constantly appeared in shows all over the eastern United States as characters such as Jumping Jack Flash, the Chocolate Playboy, the Iraqi Assassin, and Sgt Sy Youngblood. Even though my career is now over, one thing is for sure: I will always treasure the experience of enthralling audiences and assuming different personas.

I vividly recall an incident when I had a match, and I was waiting in the ring for it to begin. In the meantime, while I was praying, I overheard someone in the crowd calling me a racist slur that,

*"You are nothing but a nigger in a sheet."*

When I glanced outside the ring, two men gestured to another one who grinned toothily and acknowledged having said it. The legendary Bucky Palermo, the referee, rushed over to confront me, not to give a reprimand but to impart wisdom. He reminded me that there would be difficulties in portraying a character from the Middle East in West Virginia.

Bucky reminded me that the crowd paid for my performance and advised me not to leave the ring by myself. He told me to grow a thick skin and promised to come with me if I needed it. I'll always be grateful for Bucky's support and guidance because he was the best; he helped me understand the intricacies of the wrestling world and make sense of it all. I had a great deal of joy performing in wrestling, and I had met famous celebrities like "The Rock," Dwayne Johnson when he was a college student, and his father, Rocky Johnson, who was a promoter in the Catskills, New York. Legends like Bruno Sammartino, The Bushwackers, Jimmy "Superfly" Snuka, who gave me great advice, and the Iron Sheik were all part of my special moments. I won titles: I was crowned the Junior Heavyweight Champion of the Tri-State Wrestling Alliance, the Tri-State Tag Team Champions alongside TC Reynolds, the IWA Heavyweight Championship in Columbus, Ohio, and finally the United States Wrestling Federation Heavyweight Championship in Elmira, New York. There were many memorable interactions along the way and noteworthy wins in the wrestling world.

Even though I became well-known in the days before social media in the wrestling industry, multiple concussions ended my career. I entirely blame myself for my early departure, which came about as a result of taking significant risks in the ring just as I was starting to settle into my groove. That was the first time I really struggled with depression. I physically neglected myself, gave up weightlifting, and toiled with the emotional fallout from ending my pro wrestling career too soon. The lack of resolution and the impact on my psychological state became apparent. Indeed, it was a difficult and challenging stage of my life.

# Chapter 3: Hollywood on the Monongahela

When I began my journey at a wrestling school in Connecticut, one of the first lessons was mastering the art of falling. I arrived at the training center and noticed a jar of aspirins on the ring mat.

The trainer, Tony, emphasized the importance of learning to take bumps, explaining that it's critical for preventing injuries. He stressed the significance of tucking in your chin when falling to avoid neck injuries, explaining that distributing the shock of the fall throughout the body was essential. If you hear only one impact, it indicates a proper fall, as opposed to two impacts, which could lead to injuries, he said.

The jar of aspirins on the ring apron represented the harsh reality of the training process. Learning to fall correctly was the foundation of our training, as it prepared you for the physical demands of professional wrestling, akin to stunt work.

For the first few weeks, the only thing to practice was falling. Tony's advice was similar to that of a stuntman, *'It's crucial to comprehend the physics of a fall. Being a better stuntman is not the goal; rather, it is to make sure that moves are performed safely in the ring.'* The first few days were really difficult as I became aware of the physical toll it was taking on my body from having to get out of bed. The demanding physical requirements highlighted how important it is to grasp the fundamentals.

I can say this with certainty: the lessons I learned about falling have proven invaluable throughout my wrestling career. It's not just about executing flashy moves in the ring but understanding the basics, ensuring one's safety, and ultimately delivering a captivating performance for the audience. In the world of professional wrestling, the wrestling ring is not a trampoline, as some might assume. Early in my career, I disliked taking significant falls. Later, I got to know that the ring's condition plays a key role—some are more forgiving, while others are stiff. This influences the type of moves wrestlers dare to perform.

Essentially, the ring's responsiveness dictated the style of the match. A flexible ring encouraged riskier, acrobatic displays, while a rigid one led to a more conservative approach, prioritizing the wrestlers' well-being in a physically demanding profession.

In wrestling, the quality of the ring is crucial. If it's good, you're willing to do everything – be it diving off the top rope, suplexes, you name it. A responsive ring makes these moves safer for your body, whereas a hard ring makes you hesitant to take risks. The assessment happens after the first match, and if the ring feels good, wrestlers go all out, knowing it supports their bumps and falls.

Thus, if the ring felt good, those in the first match would report back, and I'd inquire about the "bump" quality. A favorable response meant I'd incorporate more high-flying maneuvers, trusting the ring's cushioning. However, if the ring was stiff, caution prevailed.

The process involved communication among wrestlers. Sometimes, you'd know the ring's condition from your partner—one should never forget that safety is paramount, even when pushing boundaries. It's about finding the sweet spot, particularly a ring that allows for an exciting performance without compromising the wrestlers' well-being. Careful evaluation is needed to ensure safe execution of moves in the ring. They should be thrilling yet carried out with precision in mind.

***

There have been numerous people and countless incidents during my wrestling career that were worth remembering. However, one personality that stood out was that of my buddy, Errol Siegel, a wrestling manager for the guys. He played a vital role in the wrestling family.

He managed everyone, including the good guys in the band, with his station wagon being the transport for shows. Despite our cultural differences – him being Jewish and me Arabic – we joked that if we could get along, people of our backgrounds should too. Errol, nearing 400 pounds, consistently clarified his weight as 399.5 pounds whenever I playfully brought up the larger number.

Everything in the wrestling world used to be staged. Errol Siegel, known in the wrestling world as Dr. Sam Siegel, played the role of a neurosurgeon for the criminally insane. He entered the ring with a stethoscope, establishing himself as a notorious character. Despite the theatrical persona, Errol was more than a wrestling manager; he became a dear family friend. Errol's unique character extended beyond the ring; he might have been a heavyweight, but his agility surprised many. In the world of professional wrestling, he was popularly known as a manager and a beloved friend to many. Our connection extended beyond the ring – he knew my family and my kids, and I was acquainted with his parents in New Jersey. Errol and I developed a close bond, making his death a profound and saddening moment for me. His legacy in the wrestling world remains, but the personal connection we shared was what truly makes his memory enduring and meaningful.

As a heel manager, he always handled the bad guys. Wrestling against him, especially facing young blood, meant being on the opposite side. Errol's punches were heavy-handed, lacking finesse, and when you got hit hard, it was termed getting "potatoed." I'd often tell him he was the stiffest guy around because of his forceful hits. Despite this, he and I shared a special friendship.

Chasing him around the ring became a routine, and surprisingly, for a man of his size, he was remarkably light on his feet. We bonded over the logistics of wrestling, with me driving his station wagon that transported six or seven wrestlers along with our gear. This became our mobile wrestling hub, moving us from place to place, especially when I was still new to the wrestling scene. Those journeys were filled with beautiful moments as we shared stories and laughter, forming bonds that would last a lifetime.

Early in my wrestling career, I was green and inexperienced; however, our friendship created a fraternity-like atmosphere. We became a tight-knit family, knowing each other's personal lives, wives, and families. Despite performing against each other in the ring, there was an unspoken rule – never hurt each other. Wrestling was a team effort akin to a carefully choreographed dance. The audience was our audience, and we needed to entertain them without causing harm. It was critical to be mindful of each other's well-being, ensuring that the performance remained both captivating and safe. With time, I realized wrestling was more than a sport; it was an art form. It united individuals from diverse backgrounds, turning them into a closeknit family that surpassed cultural and personal differences. There was a bunch of us, and when we would hang out together, some of the guys would smoke weed. We'd always look out for one another and warn them of the potential danger that lurked.

***

Over my wrestling career, I have created a lot of priceless memories. One of those unforgettable incidents involved the great wrestler, T.C. Reynolds, when we traveled to a show in Conneaut, Ohio, only to find it got canceled due to heavy snow. We were stranded in a Best Western motel for three days; TC had brought his son along, which created an unexpected bonding experience.

During those days, the three of us formed a unique camaraderie. TC's son, full of enthusiasm, turned the hotel room into an impromptu wrestling arena. He would leap off the furniture, performing playful elbow smashes on the bed. Despite our on-screen personas as adversaries, this time together showcased our genuine care and respect for one another.

We were more than just opponents outside the ring as we shared a close bond of companionship. This experience highlighted the deep kinship that existed among the wrestlers. We shared a bond that went beyond the scripted rivalries and emphasized sportsmanship and mutual respect. Throughout my career, I have heard of a number of false beliefs about my profession. One of the most common misconceptions people have about professional wrestlers is that they make a lot of money. However, the bitter reality is professional wrestling wasn't always lucrative for us. Some matches paid as little as 25 or 30 bucks, challenging the delusion that all wrestlers earned big money. In reality, we often earned just enough to contribute towards Errol's gas money for the journey.

Financial struggles were common, evident in the fact that sometimes we couldn't afford hotel rooms. After a show, we'd drive back to a city at night rather than staying overnight. Despite the meager pay, we maintained a sense of camaraderie. If someone was driving, others pitched in to share the responsibility.

Money was tight, and our post-match meals were often just homemade sandwiches. Breaking into the wrestling business came with financial challenges, and the initial pay didn't reflect the hard work and dedication. It was a tough journey, but the passion for wrestling and the bond among wrestlers kept us going, even in the face of financial limitations.

In professional wrestling, earnings varied, with some making 50 bucks or less per match. The promoter discreetly handed out individual payments, making it a private matter. In spite of potential disparities in pay, we never discussed who made how much, as it was considered taboo in the wrestling world.

Sometimes, I feel that wrestlers are no less than actors because we were also expected to play certain roles and remain in that character throughout the duration of our shows. Maintaining the act was essential, even offstage. Even though the good and bad guys would travel in the same car, as we reached the town, we would part ways. The "heels" (villains) would cover their faces to uphold the tradition of keeping good guys and bad guys separate. This commitment to the wrestling business's traditions extended beyond the ring, emphasizing the importance of staying in character and preserving the illusion of rivalries. It was a silent understanding among wrestlers, reinforcing the belief that both in and out of the ring, the lines between heroes and villains should remain distinct. It contributed to the mystique of professional wrestling.

We had to hide when we reached the auditorium or gym, and we would walk in separately as if we were not together five minutes ago. We worked quite hard to ensure that this secret of the business was protected at all costs. The term used for this act was "Kayfabe," meaning "be fake."

In professional wrestling, "kayfabe" was our guiding principle – the art of maintaining the illusion that wrestling was real. The separation between good guys (baby faces) and bad guys (heels) was vital to the show's success. This commitment to tradition was necessary, especially in the earlier days when audiences believed wrestling was genuine, not staged, as they now understand.

I have a fond memory of a match I worked with T.C. Reynolds, where I acted as the Iraqi assassin against his American Patriot persona. The match initially got canceled due to snow, but when rescheduled, TC won. In a planned post-match attack, I was to strike him with my Iraqi flag. TC insisted I hit him hard for authenticity. The crowd, believing in the storyline, went wild as I delivered a strong whack, leaving a diagonal mark on his back.

The reaction from the audience was intense. I had to fight my way out of the ring and escape to the dressing room. The upset promoter quickly organized two deputy sheriffs to escort me out due to safety concerns. The crowd, though supportive of my character, was genuinely furious about the flag attack. It was a unique experience where I learned about the power of storytelling in wrestling and how emotionally invested the audience could get.

Being a heel, the "bad guy," was more enjoyable for me as it always brought excitement. Stirring up the crowd, triggering reactions, and saying things to get them riled up added a dynamic aspect to the performance. However, this particular incident took it to another level, as the audience got outraged. While the promoter appreciated the crowd's reaction, he was genuinely concerned for my safety, leading to the escort by deputy sheriffs out of town.

The intensity of the crowd's reaction, the heat I generated, was a testament to the success of the performance. Yet, it came at the cost of my safety, revealing the fine line wrestlers walked between entertainment and personal risk. It was a clear indicator that, as a villain, I had done an effective job if the crowd believed the events were real. Despite the dangers, it highlighted the immersive nature of professional wrestling, where the audience's emotional investment exceeded the scripted nature of the matches.

As I quickly showered and dressed, the sheriffs ushered me out of town. The adrenaline, mixed with the genuine concern for my well-being, made it a memorable and somewhat harrowing experience. It was a stark reminder that the commitment to kayfabe occasionally had tangible consequences. In retrospect, the incident remains a vivid chapter in my wrestling journey. It reflects the unique dynamics between performers and the audience, where the illusion of reality is carefully maintained. It can create an exhilarating spectacle that can, at times, spill beyond the boundaries of the ring. The passion, both from the performers and the audience, was what made professional wrestling an enduring and remarkable form of entertainment.

The promoter of our shows looked like he could be cast in The Sopranos, like he owned a chain of pizza shops around Youngstown, Ohio. He always appreciated my Middle Eastern gimmick, recognizing it as a compelling element for the audience. However, despite his enthusiasm, there was a genuine concern for my safety after a particularly intense match with Tommy that night.

The blurred lines between fiction and reality were evident as the audience, fully invested in the storyline, was ready to break down doors to reach the locker room where I was. Despite the controlled chaos in the ring, the camaraderie among wrestlers remained strong. Once out of the town and away from the fervent audience, we would regroup, sharing meals and laughs with each other.

***

My wrestling career proved to be quite adventurous for me as I was also given a chance to be cast in multiple movies as an extra. During a show in Pittsburgh, I was at a bar called Harris Grill. It was run by a Greek family, and it was the same place where I met my second wife.  An unexpected turn of events during a tour led me to the world of acting. A bartender working at the venue where we performed happened to be associated with Nancy Mosser Casting Agency; it was known for casting extras in movies. Intrigued by the idea, she arranged an interview for me, considering my unique background in professional wrestling.

This opportunity opened doors for me to be part of several movies, including "Silence of the Lambs." Initially, there was a chance for a more visible role with the SWAT team, but a clash emerged over my long bleach-blonde hair. The producers wanted me to cut it for authenticity, even though the part didn't include any speaking lines or eligibility for a Screen Actors Guild (SAG) card. Unwilling to compromise my wrestling gimmick, I declined, leading to a less prominent scene with Jodie Foster at a Pittsburgh airport where I stood in a corner.

The situation repeated in "Lorenzo's Oil," where I secured a more visible part as an extra. However, the clash over my appearance occurred again in "Dead and Alive: The Race for Gus Farace," featuring stars like Tony Danza and a rising actor named Samuel L. Jackson. I did not agree with what the producers wanted me to do with my hair.

During the same trip, in a memorable encounter with Samuel L. Jackson during a meal break, he expressed disdain for the catering food, calling it "MFN shit." Playing the role of a smart aleck, I suggested we go to his trailer for better food, eliciting laughs from fellow extras. Although Jackson shot me a stern look, he walked away without responding. Little did I know that he would become a highly sought - after actor in the years to come. Even though I have had my fair share of challenges during my wrestling career, it was a fun journey. In a phase of my life marked by diverse experiences, my involvement in professional wrestling became intertwined with unexpected ventures into acting and modeling. This multifaceted journey unfolded during a vibrant period in Pittsburgh when film productions thrived and opportunities seemed boundless.

Initially transitioning from the Military to civilian life, I found myself driving a cab with the distinctive number 225, known to listeners of Ron Chavis's nighttime radio show. This unexpected exposure became a unique form of promotion, providing a pleasant push for my endeavors. While wrestling consumed my weekends, cab driving sustained me during the week, offering financial stability.

In this dynamic phase, I pursued a private investigation school, unveiling a diverse blend of professions. My days were a whirlwind of wrestling matches, movie roles, and modeling assignments. I embraced every opportunity, relishing the thrill of living out dreams conceived during my teenage years. This period, precluding my second marriage, offered a carefree existence where the stresses of family life hadn't yet materialized.

Amid the excitement, I delved into a wrestling match, recounting incidents that underscored the inherent risks in this physically demanding sport. One particular match in upstate New York left me with a foggy memory after a potentially dangerous move. Despite the grogginess, the show went on, illustrating the adrenaline-fueled determination that characterized live performances. However, the pinnacle of risk unfolded during a match in Batavia, NY, with Larry Winters. I will elaborate on this incident later in the chapter. Wrestling through the pain, the match concluded, but it marked a turning point. The cumulative toll of concussions and injuries reached a critical juncture, prompting concern from my doctor. Facing a pivotal decision, I had to acknowledge the physical toll of my wrestling career. The inherent risks, from concussions to broken ribs, were undeniable.

Even though I had suffered a severe injury and my second wife, doctor, and promoter wanted me to shorten the tour, I denied it. I went to the ring again and battled in a tag team match. There was a gentleman wrestler, Muhammad Abdullah, who was from Sudan and lived on the north side of Pittsburgh. He was like a brother to me, and it was a match against him that led to severe injuries.

During the match, he threw me into a turnbuckle and charged at me; he accidentally got my ribs, and we both heard them crack. He felt terrible as soon as he made the move since he could see I was unable to breathe after that. My tag team partner then came in and finished the match on my behalf, as I could not continue due to my wounds.

I remember when my fingers were dislocated, the referee, with an eagle eye, surprisingly came in to help me snap them back into place. For some reason, I shared a strange bond with him. If I was playing "baby face" in a match, he would support the "heel guy" and vice versa. He was quite an experienced referee and taught me much throughout my wrestling career.

Reflecting on these incidents, I recognized the contrast between professional wrestling and the myths that followed. It is often dismissed as "fake" due to its scripted nature, yet it remains undeniably grueling and physically demanding. The story encapsulates the paradox of an industry that combines athleticism with showmanship, where performers navigate a delicate balance between entertainment and genuine physical risk.

Another incident that left an impression on me is one with the living legend Larry Winters. It brought about a whirlwind of wrestling shows, with five events packed into four intense days. The tour began on a Thursday night, followed by Friday night, Saturday afternoon, and Saturday evening, which concluded with a Sunday afternoon show. Such rigorous schedules were common on the independent wrestling circuit, demanding physical resilience and an unwavering commitment to the craft.

The specific incident that looms large in my memory occurred in Batavia, State, New York, during this tour. The wrestling shows were strategically timed, combining early afternoon and evening performances: a format that tested the limits of physical endurance. Despite the challenges, we, as professional wrestlers, thrived on the opportunity to showcase our skills and entertain audiences.

The focal point of this tour was the memorable match with Larry Winters, where an ill-fated insistence on executing a piledriver became a pivotal moment in my wrestling career. Larry had reservations about the move's potential dangers, expressing reluctance to proceed. However, fueled by determination and perhaps underestimating the risks, I urged him to press on. This specific match was not just an ordinary part of the tour but a culmination of events leading to a defining moment. At its core, wrestling involves calculated risks, and sometimes these risks can result in injuries. In this instance, the repercussions were severe, leaving a part of my scalp exposed due to the piledriver. Broken ribs from a poorly executed move caused my fingers to dislocate fingers, as well as other injuries. This painted a vivid picture of the physical demands the ring required.

The rigors of the tour continued despite the physical toll. Indeed, wrestlers often find themselves caught between the adrenaline-fueled determination to entertain the audience and the undeniable strains on their bodies. So, as I grappled with the aftermath of the piledriver incident, the show persisted. There was no ceremonial retirement match or a chance to bid farewell on my terms.

A wrestler often envisions a grand exit, a retirement match, or a ceremonious farewell, a luxury that eluded me. Wrestling, a profession that encapsulates the highs of triumph and the lows of injury, demanded that I confront the reality of an unplanned departure.

Despite the abrupt end to my wrestling career, recognition and appreciation followed. Induction into the Hall of Fame of the United States Wrestling Federation validated the impact of my contributions. This acknowledgment extended beyond the ring as I engaged with the community. Talks at Boys and Girls Clubs, hospital visits to inspire children, and promotional events became integral to my role as a champion.

Being the spokesperson for the United States Wrestling Federation went beyond in-ring performances. It involved radio promos, TV appearances, and community engagement. The responsibility of upholding the tradition and promoting the organization fell on the champion, providing an opportunity to inspire and motivate through various avenues. The postwrestling phase saw a full-circle journey as I transitioned into motivational speaking and mentoring, mainly focusing on youth. The impact on children during Boys and Girls Club visits illustrated the profound influence wrestlers can have beyond the confines of the ring. Wrestling, often misunderstood as scripted entertainment, becomes a powerful platform for mentors and motivators to connect with impressionable minds.

# Chapter 4: Losing Part Of My Soul

I remember I had a severe concussion from my wrestling match in Batavia, New York. Upon my return to my family's home in Alexandria, Virginia, I decided to discuss my injuries with my doctor. He was aware of my history of concussions and that I was a professional wrestler. He cautioned me against wrestling any longer, especially after having multiple jolts.

My doctor explained one more serious concussion could have been lethal or caused a traumatic brain injury. Given the risks, he felt obligated to advise me to no longer wrestle. I became aware of how serious the situation was after hearing him speak. Despite this advice, I wrestled in one final show in Sullivan County, New York.

I decided to retire quietly without telling anyone after that match. I shook hands with everyone, left the wrestling world behind, and went back to Virginia to take care of my family and health because I didn't want to risk getting hurt anymore.

I attended one more wrestling show in New York despite my doctor's warnings about the dangers of carrying on with the sport due to the concussions. I had already committed to the event, so I took the risk; however, after that show, I felt it was time to call it quits. My wife and the promoter were among those who were disappointed that there was no formal ceremony to mark my retirement. My wife was worried about the potential effects on our family should I suffer another concussion; hence, they were all worried about my safety. It was difficult for me to retire from professional wrestling because I missed the excitement of competing. It was impossible to describe the sensation of hearing the crowd react or walk through the door with my music playing. Their applause and jeers gave me a rush of excitement, and I really missed the energy I got from their adoration.

Leaving wrestling behind caused me to disregard my physical well-being. I stopped exercising, put on weight, and drank too much; it was a physically and emotionally taxing time for me. I was upset that I was unable to retire at my own will; rather, it was because of events beyond my control.

However, after I quit wrestling, my security career took off, which comforted me. I was able to move on and adjust to the changes in my life in spite of the challenges. Even though I missed the ring's thrill, I was content in other areas of my work as I was doing well.

I am glad I made beautiful memories throughout my career that I will cherish for the rest of my life. I remember the time I wrestled in the Civic Arena in Pittsburgh in front of 10,000 fans; it was an exhilarating experience.

It was exciting to wrestle in front of a large audience, especially since so many of my friends were also there to watch the show. We already knew we would lose the match because it was preplanned, but that did not lessen the thrill. We faced off against the legendary tag team, the original Midnight Express. I looked good with my partner, Dante DiNucci, but my bodybuilding friends didn't get why we had to lose to them. They were unaware of the fact that these performances used to be scripted. The promoter and booker would decide who would win the match, and we were only informed. At that time, the National Wrestling Alliance became the WCW and was quite well known. It was competing against the WWF, which later became the WWE. It was an NWA show that I was on, but there were a lot of top names, like Lex Luger and Ric Flair, in WCW.

That night in the Civic Arena was one of the highlights of my wrestling career, even though I was disappointed to lose. The crowd's energy was amazing, especially in the packed 10,000person arena. It was deafening! It was an incredible rush to perform in front of such a big audience and to feel their enthusiasm. These kinds of occasions make all the effort and sacrifice worthwhile.

In addition to wrestling, I got to tour the Midwest for four shows with the band Steppenwolf. At county fairs, they would watch us wrestle in the afternoon, and we would watch them (Steppenwolf) play their concert at night. It was fantastic! My wrestling career has given me so much to be thankful for.

Giving up on wrestling was certainly like losing a part of my soul. Having devoted 16 years to professional wrestling—I even left the Air Force in 1986 to pursue it—I felt incredibly let down. Wrestling was my passion, even though I could have continued in the Military and had a retirement plan. It was a big blow to leave wrestling, even though I later returned to the Military briefly.

I enjoyed every aspect of wrestling, including the travel, the buddy relationships with the guys, and even giving inspirational speeches at Boys and Girls Clubs. Although it was rewarding to represent the sport, I always thought I could have reached a wider audience if social media had been available. I would have had more access to a larger platform if social media had been there back then. Regardless of my efforts, I did not get the widespread exposure I could have had in today's world. Having no one to talk to about this disappointment made it even more difficult to deal with.

I became aware of changes in myself after giving up wrestling. My already heavy drinking further worsened, and I put on weight. I wasn't angry at anyone in particular; I was just disappointed in the situation I found myself in. I felt helpless because things had gotten to a point where a doctor had to intervene.

*** 

In 2000, while I was in the Washington DC area, I received a call from a company called the Potomac Group based in Alexandria, Virginia. They asked me to provide security for a workplace situation in southern Virginia. It turned out the company was shutting down, and I was tasked with protecting the vice president, who had to deliver the news. I did a good job, and word quickly spread about my abilities.

Soon, I gained a nickname: "the king of the dot com closures." You see, the dot com industry was crashing at that time, and many high-tech companies were leaving the business. I would be called in to oversee the closures, ensuring they were carried out smoothly and safely. My military background and discipline helped me excel in this role.

My reputation for meticulous and thorough work grew as the requests for these closures continued. People started referring me for security assignments because they could trust my experience. My career in the DC area's security industry started because of this. Eventually, I started doing international travel for work and had already been to 40 countries by then. However, as I became more well-known in the security industry, I discovered that I was traveling even more. I started providing security for international events like the Olympics, requiring me to travel to many nations. As of now, I guess I have been to 136 countries, and in my opinion, South Africa is definitely one of the best places to travel. Cape Town is among my top five favorite cities worldwide: New York, Rio De Janeiro, Melbourne, and Bangkok.

I developed a prosperous career in security by being committed and professional, which helped me gain the respect and trust of my coworkers. I excelled in this field because of the discipline and attention to detail my military training imparted. Even though it was difficult for me to leave professional wrestling, it helped me have a successful career in security.

It's true that initially, I was devastated at my decision to opt out of wrestling; however, as time passed, I made peace with it. I realized that nothing in this life is permanent, and we should accept this reality. Life does not stop and goes on no matter what; we must learn to live with it. There's always light at the end of the tunnel, so we should never lose hope during tough times.

# Chapter 5: Fatherhood

One of the most rewarding aspects of this life is fatherhood. Watching your kids grow into promising and talented individuals is an unmatched joy. Seeing their first steps, hearing their first words, and witnessing their unique personalities blossom are moments that stay with you forever. It is truly a blessing that I was lucky enough to be blessed with. My three kids are the light of my life, and I can easily sacrifice my life for them.

My beautiful firstborn, Tasha Nycole Alli, is from my first wife, Vielka Johnson. Vielka and I married at a very young age. She was 18, and I was 21, and we thought we knew everything in the world. Our decision seemed like the most sensible thing to do as we were two young people in love.

Salli Sy Alli Jr., my father, was not fond of this idea. He tried to make me see things from the long-run perspective and advised me not to be hasty with such a pivotal decision. He tried to explain how both of us were young and we needed to explore ourselves further at that age. However, at that age, we were quite immature and went along with what felt right to us. My father, God, rest his soul. Even after disagreeing in the beginning, he understood our decision and extended his blessings.

In 1982, Vielka and I got married at a Justice of The Peace in Minot, North Dakota. There was no church, no big wedding dinner, no speeches, just two people having made a decision to spend their lives together. Everything seemed blissful initially, and we mostly lived in Germany as I was deployed there. In 1984, our beautiful daughter Tasha was born. The base hospital at Hahn

Air Base lacked bed space, and we needed family support, given that I was on duty for an assignment that spanned over a month. Her parents were in California, and we urgently booked a flight there. It was a good decision because her parents helped at the time of Tasha's birth, although parting with my partner at such an emotionally charged time was quite difficult for me.

As soon as my assignment ended, I flew out to California. I could not wait to hold my precious angel and be near my partner. I immediately fell in love with Tasha. She had the face of an Egyptian doll baby with big doe eyes. I was happy beyond compare. Her slightly Arabic features and angelic face had my heart in its grip. The emotions that I felt at the birth of my children cannot be compared with any other feeling. Truly, fatherhood is a blessing.

After Tasha's birth, I left the Military to pursue a career in wrestling and become a professional wrestler. This is where Veilka and I had our disagreement. She wanted me to stay in the Military as I had a bright future ahead of me. I was successfully climbing up the ranks and was very well respected as a supervisor and mentor. However, my penchant for wrestling was too strong, and in 1987, Veilka and I separated our paths.

It was a tough time in life. I had lost my partner and, inevitably, my daughter too. The role of a father that I could have performed by being there for Tasha, I was unable to. Luckily, my bond with my daughter over the years remained strong. The credit for this strong connection also goes to Veilka, who raised our daughter well and always kept me a part of Tasha's life, especially at a younger age. Looking back at it, Veilka and I laugh at the decision we made at such a young age. We were both immature, but she was definitely more mature than me even then. I am one of those lucky people who have cordial relations with their former partners. There is no animosity between us. To Veilka, I will always wish success and happiness for the wonderful human that she is.

Sometimes, life has a way of teaching us new lessons that, at the time, we are unable to grasp the enormity of. We resent and question, but with time, we understand that we go through various situations only to reach a better place, which is life's gift to us. It is also always important to remember that no destination in life is the final destination. Life goes on, and you should go along with it.

The lesson that I learned from my first marriage was that when you are young and immature, you also tend to be selfish. It happens to everyone, but what matters is overcoming that tendency and striving to become a better version of yourself. In my case, it took a little longer but only aided in making me the person I am now.

On the 3rd of September, 1994, I married my second wife, Alicia George. She was a successful woman working as a TV news executive, and I was in love with her. Alicia and I had two beautiful children together. Samaria Hope Alli, who we called Sammie, was born on the 30th of January 1996, and her little brother, Sy Salli Alli the Fourth, came into this world on the 11th of October 2000.

Due to my deployment, I missed Tasha's birth at the time, but with Sammie and Sy, I was able to witness the miracle of the birth of your child. No words can ever encapsulate the feeling of watching your child being born and realizing that you are a parent now. Events like these have a long-lasting impact on your heart and mind, and they completely alter your life.

As Alicia worked in television, I tried to limit my traveling to professional wrestling as we had little Sammie with us. She needed her parents, and with both out of the picture, the child would have been completely neglected. I had offers for tours all around the world, but it didn't sit well with me to leave the complete responsibility of our child on my wife, especially when she worked full time as well.

So, after 16 years in professional wrestling, I left it and started working in the Security industry. I was utterly broken. Wrestling was my dream and my passion. Unfortunately, I had to let it go, and these traumatic changes started setting the tone for my second marriage. As an escape, I drowned myself in work.

I wanted to be present; I wanted to be there with my family, my wife and kids, but I could not. During a couple of years with my job in the security industry, I was on the road for 250 days a year, and that is a significant amount of time away from your loved ones. The people close to you don't deserve your absence. As a partner and a parent, you must always prioritize them and appreciate their presence.

However, Alicia was a patient woman, and she didn't give up on our marriage. However, our relationship really hit rock bottom when I retreated. After my father died in 2005, and a little later, my father-in-law, I was completely grief-stricken and lost. I submerged myself in work and traveling. I grew increasingly distant from my family, and instead of seeking counsel, I became more rigid in my ways. I didn't seek help. I didn't trust my partner and marriage when I should have done exactly that. Sharing your happiness and grievances in a marriage is very important, I now believe, as it allows trust and companionship to flow through your relationship, and both partners feel included in each other's life.

And so it happened that the depression took the best of me. I spent months on the road, absent from everyone's lives, and eventually, I had to face the consequences. In 2014, Alicia and I separated ways. We were married for 20 years and were involved for six years before that. To know a person for 26 years and then to lose them... the pain was incomprehensible, and I didn't know how to function.

To grieve when you don't know how to is the hardest part of life. You wake up, and you feel a burden on your soul, but you are unable to unburden yourself. In 2015, I gave in to weakness and tried to end my life. However, in times like these, one must always remember that there is always a warm summer after a harsh winter. You must always seek guidance and counseling so that you don't fight your battles alone like I tried to.

Alicia was an amazing woman and my partner for a very long time. My own shortcomings made us part ways. Through the outcome of my marriages, I was able to self-analyze myself and work on becoming a better person. This path led me to where I am today: more spiritually grounded.

Both my marriages provided me with the blessing of fatherhood. Watching Tasha, Sammie, and Sy makes me beam with pride. They all grew up to be wonderful and talented people.

My former partners worked relentlessly with the children, even at times when I was occupied with work. The adults, all three of them, have grown, and the bond of love that they share with each other fills my heart with joy and warmth.

Tasha, who will be hitting 40 soon, is a mother herself to my 3-year-old granddaughter, Joiee Wray Kenney. She and I share a very strong father-daughter bond, and this bond has only grown stronger as I have matured with age.

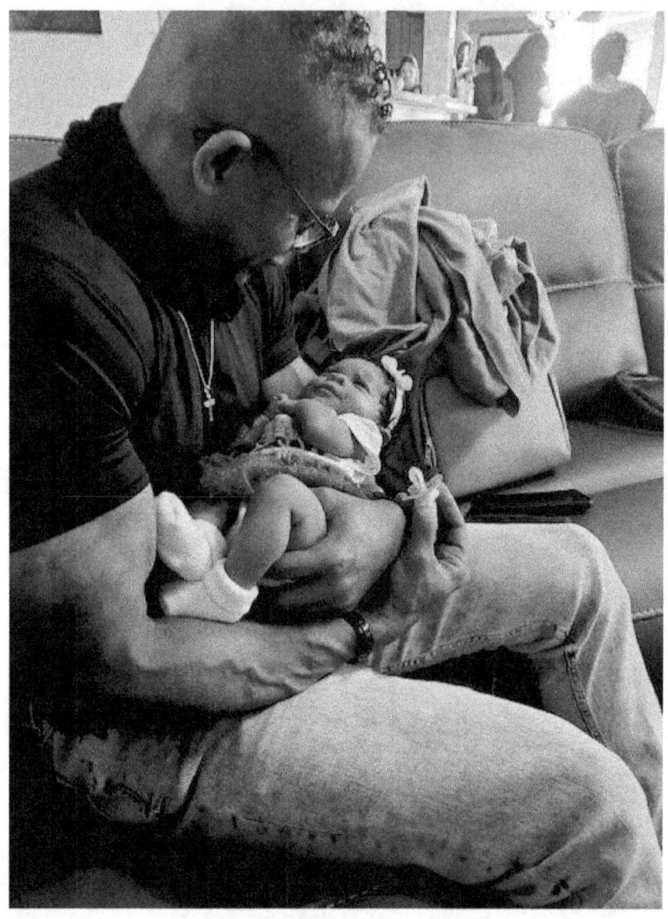

Samaria, who is 27, is a professional woman working in a private jet company in Arizona. She works in the logistical department and likes to venture around. She has inherited her nomadic tendencies from me. While Tasha looks just like me, Samaria is just like me.

My little boy, Sy the Fourth, is not little anymore, either. He is 23 years old and a professional football player in Mexico. He is a beautiful athlete and an even more beautiful soul. During my divorce from Alicia, while Samaria was busy settling down and college, Sy was alone. He was deeply hurt and upset. However, even after everything, he and I share an unbreakable bond, and I am unquestionably proud of him. In the place I am at, I have found solace and built a connection with God. I don't sit and lament my past. I have made my mistakes and learned my lessons. I wish that I was a more present father and partner, but unfortunately, I was not.

However, I have worked on that and tried to be there for my children and celebrate their lives. Not only do I try to be a better father to Tasha, but I also try to be an amazing grandfather to little Joiee.

The key to life is always to start small and move on to bigger things. This promises changes that are irreversible. I took baby steps; I controlled my habit of cursing and then eventually stopped altogether. Then, I targeted my habit of drinking and then, smoking. In the long run, I overcame the habits that I attributed to my weakness and proved to my children that I was making an effort. In life, there are many hard times that you will face and many dreams that you might have to give up on. Still, it is important to remember that some dreams do come true.

As a young boy, I dreamt of being a superhero, and I did. I lived my dream of professional wrestling; that was nothing less than being a superhero. Now that God has taken me under His wing, I cannot thank the forces enough for letting my journey lead me here. I am much older and wiser now, with my heart at peace. My children might not understand my decision to become a minister yet, but I know both Veilka and Alicia appreciate it. It is always important to follow your heart; the rest follows.

# Chapter 6: Farewell my Friend

My father, Salli Sy Alli Jr., was part Arabic since my grandfather was from Yemen. He had big eyes that would penetrate deep into your soul. When he used to get angry, his big eyes would open wide like a drill sergeant. On the outside, my father was a tough man with whom anybody would think twice before messing with. However, on the inside, he was a soft man with a soft heart.

He was a beloved figure in the community. Everybody simply adored my father. Back in his day, he was a legendary high school basketball player, the star of the show. He was so good at his game that he could have been playing with Harlem Globetrotters. His par-excellence performance at the game even earned him a heroic position.

A famous incident about my father's exceptional sports skills that I grew up listening to was that he shot at the buzzer, which was a monumental moment. He was in high school back then and wanted to secure a place for his team in the state championship. During my high school years, I was always told that I take after my father in sports, and now, so does my son, Sy the Fourth.

Every child's dream is to have their fathers accompany them to their games. My beloved father made that dream come true. He would often accompany me to basketball and play with me and my friends. My friends admired him deeply and, at the same time, adored him as well. He was a man who could make his place in anyone's heart.

Along with his passion for basketball, he was also well-known in the community as a mailman. He was a well-respected man who had connections with everyone. His kind heart made him popular and almost everyone's favorite. As a child, I loved accompanying my father on Saturdays to go and deliver mail.

In the mornings, we used to go to the post office first. There, we used to sort out the mail while he and I chatted. Then, we would get into his jeep, and off he would go delivering mail all around. It was a fun time. Even after years, I hold it close to my heart. Looking back, as a child, it was one of those moments that set the foundations of my strong relationship with him. When I was around eight years old, my parents had a falling out. They could no longer work their way together, so they parted ways. As a young child, I did not understand what was happening. It escaped me as to why my mother no longer lived with us. My sister and I moved in with our dad while our mom moved back home to Pittsburgh.

Growing up, I never held any form of animosity against my mother. She held a very special place in our hearts and lives.

However, I was confused. I could not grasp the concept of divorce, but my father was a strong man and held onto us throughout the whole process and after. As children, you often tend to blame yourself for the turbulence in your parents' lives.

You question their love for you and the place you hold in their lives. There are a lot of 'whys' that start haunting your little mind, but my father was a strong man. He assured my sister and me, in every possible way, that we were not at fault. He paid special attention to details and made sure that we did not grow up blaming ourselves in any way. He was present in our lives every step of the way, and thus, our bond with him never wavered; it remained as strong as it was in our childhoods.

In life, there are moments that you never expect or at least hope that you will never get to see. One of those possibilities that you pray will not affect your life even when you see people around you going through them. For me, it was when my father was diagnosed with colon cancer. My world was ripped from under my feet. I almost felt like I would lose my footing.

However, in those intricate instances, you should remain strong. You should become a wall for others to rest their heads upon. When my father was diagnosed with a life-threatening disease, I pulled myself together and stepped up on his behalf. I took him to chemotherapy sessions regularly while I waited outside for him.

Undoubtedly, it was a dark time. Waiting is always difficult in life. It keeps your hope alive, and you fixate on the idea of a nascent sun that will illuminate your life and pull you out of the darkness. For me, I hoped for my father to make it while I waited in those dark corridors of the hospital. However, I knew my father was a man of strong and unshakable will and that he would make it; fight with every ounce of power he had, and miraculously he did. Sometimes, just when you think everything is over, you have survived the storm and made it to the shore, you are hurled back to the beginning. My father was in remission when the tragic news was broken to us. We got a phone call from the doctors informing us that they had detected tumors on his brain, which means that the cancer had, unfortunately, spread to his brain. To say it was hard would be an understatement, yet I still kept my hope.

The gravity of the situation dawned upon me when I heard the doctor in conversation with the nurse about my father and how he only had six months to live. It was at the nurse's station, and the doctor was unaware that I was related to the patient. I was completely caught off guard. I knew he was sick, but I never thought that he would just have a number of days left.

A backward count was set upon my father's life. It was difficult to accept that his life could now be measured in numbers. You never expect the death of your loved ones. Even after they are gone, it takes a long time before you come to terms with the harshest reality of life.

He lived in an apartment in Ohio. I remember there were no elevators where he lived, and he would get late for his appointments, so I carried him down the stairs on my back. He had grown weak and could no longer navigate, so he was given a place at the personal care home. It was one of the toughest periods of my life; watching the pillar of strength that my father crumbled right in front of my eyes completely devastated me.

Then, I did not even have my faith to keep me afloat. I was slowly internalizing all the pain and growing more distant from life. At one point in 2005, I was working for South African

Archbishop Desmond Tutu on his protection detail, and I had to be away from my father and did not know how to. I was terrified that he might pass away while I was on duty because his tumors were expanding. The strong man my father was, he still made me go to work and reassured me that he would be there when I returned.

Like a rock, here was there upon my return. I remember, in late September, I was once sitting by his hospital bedside, reading the local newspaper and narrating the football and baseball scores. It was a ritual of ours, and I thoroughly enjoyed it as I felt closer and more connected to him.

On that day, as I was reading the scores, I glanced over him, and to my surprise, he was sitting up. I was delighted because his condition was deteriorating quickly. Instantly, he met my eyes and smiled slowly. I remember what he said next because it completely caught me off guard.

He said, "You know, Sy, when you die, they should put your eyes on display in the Smithsonian." At that time, I thought that his illness had affected his cognitive skills, but he explained to me how I took for granted all my global travels and all the protection projects of influential people I have handled.

He listed all the big names I had worked for, including the former US Vice President Al Gore, former Russian President Mikhail Gorbachev, Former Secretary of State Colin Powell, Archbishop Tutu, and many more. He also expressed how amazed he was that I had traveled to 136 countries and how exceptionally lucky that makes me. At that time, it did not hit me where he was leading with it, and I told him that it was just a part of my job. However, that derailed him. He told me I was being cavalier and didn't see how fortunate I was; he said, "Sy, you are blessed but too dumb to know it." One thing that stuck with me was he said that I should be chronicling my travels for a book, and like that, my beloved father planted a seed, one week before his death, that is now sprouting.

***

During this time, I was married to my ex-wife, Alicia, and we decided to move back to Pittsburgh to be closer to family. My mom still lived there, and so did Alicia's parents. The kids got to see their grandparents, which was good for them. My sister also frequently visited us and developed a stronger bond with her nieces and nephews. My father was only an hour's drive away, which meant that we could easily reach him.

Having the support of your family in difficult times is a real blessing. You can relate to each other's experiences and navigate your way through the turbulence with someone by your side. You don't feel completely lost, and you know that there is always someone who will pull you up when you start to go under.

One by one, the day eventually came when my father passed away. That day in 2005 is still fresh in my memory, like yesterday. I watched him take his dying breath right in front of my eyes while I held onto his hand. I knew he was in great pain, that he was suffering, and that it would only relieve him and bring him peace. Yet, I wished in desperation that he could have waited a little longer, just a little more time.

Back then, I did not know how to grieve. I wanted to confide in someone and let myself loose, but I did not know how to do it.

I tried to make it through the days after his death by hiding my feelings. I presented myself strongly and supported them while never allowing anyone to support me in return. To cope with situations like these, you always go towards instant relief. I went to drinking and drowning myself with work. Instead of sitting with the loss and processing it, I tried to drink it down and forget. I was thinking from instant to instant and had completely lost sight of how deeply it would affect me in the long run.

During the grieving period, I developed a habit of calling my father's phone number. I knew that nobody would answer, but in sheer desperation, denial, and despair, I would hear his voicemail again and again. The sound of his voice was my only solace.

There are five stages of grief: denial, anger, bargaining, depression, and finally acceptance. I was in denial, and rather than going through the steps, I shut myself completely, developing unhealthy habits until I found myself in depression. I did not have a counselor, I did not have a chaplain, and for me, all alone, acceptance did not come for years.

It was only when I found Christ that I was born again. I understand the inevitable reality of life, that is, death, and how one should always think of it and accept it. Our lives are mere dots in this grand cosmos, and the phenomenon of death humbles us to accept this reality.

After the death of my father, during the period of my divorce, I understood him better as a human. It was like he had guided me on how to get through the difficult times and never let go of the children. When marriages end, both partners find themselves in vulnerable places, occupied with themselves. The children are mostly lost during this period. My father never lost sight of me and my sister. He catered to every need of ours before his own, and it was only his footsteps that I walked in when I went through the same ordeal. I tried to be there for Tasha, Sammie, and Sy, all the same.

The loss after someone's death can never be fulfilled, but it is important to remember that one must continue to live. You should always cherish the departed and celebrate them through their memories. Even as a Chaplain now, I always tell people to look back at the good memories when they are in the process of grieving and use them as their strength.

I honor my father by looking back at the fun times that my father and I spent and all the lessons that he taught me. The memories just warm my heart. Everything I achieved in life was because I knew he was always there to support and cheer me on. He was an extraordinary man and a brilliant father – *just beloved*.

# Chapter 7: Strike Two

Sometimes, life blesses you with more than what you can ask for. I was a lucky person as I was blessed with two sets of parents: my loving father, Salli Sy Alli Jr., and my mother, Joan Ann but then, I also had my in-laws, Reverend Samuel Williams George and Alethia Wilson George, who were no less than my parents.

I shared a very special relationship with my father-in-law. Calling him my father-in-law would not serve justice in our relationship because he treated me like a son. Similarly, with my mother-in-law, she catered to me like her own. It was like Heaven had opened its doors for me and blessed me with two amazing sets of people to call parents.

My father-in-law, Dad George, was a Presbyterian minister. He was born in 1922 in Sardinia, South Carolina, where he grew up. During the 30s and 40s, growing up in the South was hard due to all the political upheaval and the ongoing war.

In high school, Dad George was really into sports and was a great athlete. He played college football at Johnson C. Smith University and was outstanding at that. My son Sy inherited athletic genes from both his maternal and paternal grandfathers, which is why he is also an exceptional athlete himself.

However, Dad George never played football professionally, which could be because he went to the seminary. He was a devout Christian man and had a particular way of looking at life. However, he was an extremely tolerant man and never judged anyone. He was a true man of God, and it was thoroughly reflected in his daily actions and operations. I immensely enjoyed his company. Along with being a man of code and conduct, he also had a fantastic sense of humor. He was kind and compassionate. His beautiful soul was just a treasure to behold. For the younger people, he was a definite premier role model, while for the older, he was simply an outstanding individual.

***

I met Dad George, after seven years of dating his daughter, my ex-wife, Alicia. I had finally gathered the courage to go and ask for their permission to marry their daughter. I was intimidated as he was a well-respected minister in Pittsburgh, but his attitude toward me was extremely kind and generous, and he treated me with a lot of respect.

By the time I first met him, he had already retired from active preaching and had served as the Pastor Emeritus of Grace Memorial Presbyterian Church in Pittsburgh. He was one of the top ministers there, and I was lucky enough to witness him preach a few times. What a joy it was to behold.

Watching him was like watching a pure, principled man of God. As our relationship improved, I finally asked for their daughter's hand in marriage, and they said yes. From there on, I lucked out as I got to experience a beautiful fatherly relationship with an admirable man.

These little, intricate details about how a person carries themselves around others are what makes them a good human. He was respected by all, and that was because he extended the same courtesy to others. Dad George was a very kind man – a true gem. Dad, George, and I had an amazing time together. He was always welcoming, and we always found common ground.

He and I could sit for hours and watch football games and talk about football games. His favorite team was the Steelers; he absolutely loved them. Along with playing at Johnson C. Smith, he had also served as a coach there, so watching football with him was a treat as he knew the X's and O's of the game.

He was a strong and sturdy man, which could be majorly attributed to his intense passion for sports. Even when he was older, he would let my son side tackle him. My ex-wife, Alicia, and I would often express our worries and say, "Dad, don't let him hit you like that," but he would always retort, "That boy is not gonna hurt me."

In life, you come across very few men like Dad George. He was a physically, mentally, and spiritually strong person, and you could feel this in the energy he exuded when he was around. He was a man who would shake your hand, and you would know who you had in front of you. I knew that grip, and I will always remember the strength of his hand on my shoulder.

***

We did not always live in Pittsburgh, but before we moved, Alicia was a part of the Grace Memorial Church, and hence, when we moved back, our whole family became a part of the Church. As Dad George was a pastor there, the first and second rows used to be reserved for the family members; he would sit there with his wife, Alicia, and our kids.

Even though, back then, I did not have a connection with Christ, or at least one that I had accepted, I still, along with my children and ex-wife, played an active role in the church services.

Looking back now, I realize that there had been a pull, an influence of the Church, in my life because even then, Dad George saw something in me that I could not myself. He would always volunteer me to serve as the liturgist in Church, someone who reads the announcements and the Scripture until the pastor comes up. There is one incident that I often recall, and I wonder what a deeply observant man he was. It was a Sunday dinner, and we were all sitting together when he asked me if I would ever consider going to the seminary. At that time, I almost choked and spat out my food, and everybody except my father-in-law laughed.

With a straight face, he said, "I have seen you when you address the church, and people respond to you." He continued to tell me how there was something in my voice that would hold command in Church and that he was appreciative of how I presented myself in the Church.

However, back then, I had not taken him seriously. Simply put, I was a goofball and did not pay heed. But he must have seen something early on.

He was a God's man, and it almost felt like what he was talking about was a prophecy. At that point, I had never thought that one day I would find Christ in such a beautiful way.

For me, Dad George was very much like Christ. He was a compassionate and kind human being who was amazing with his family, friends, and everyone around.

Both he and my mother-in-law were overcome with joy when Sy and Sammie were born. They were beautiful souls, and they also accepted and loved Tasha, my daughter from my previous marriage, as their own.

They used to go out of their way to be active and present in the lives of their grandchildren. They absolutely doted over the kids as they would come to watch Sy's sports activities and matches and would also go to Sammie's piano recitals.

In all my life, I have known only a few people as kind-hearted and nice as them. Both Dad, George, and Alethia were married for 57 years, and they were both very God-oriented. I learned a lot from them regarding family values and looking after their loved ones. I learned from them how to keep my family first because I lacked in that area, but he certainly never did.

***

In 2009, Dad George passed away, four years after my father's death. I was already in a miserable condition where I kept on bottling up my emotions and did not seek help. His death was a brutal blow, and I was completely shattered as well as shocked by it. I did not know how to express my pain. I did not know how to talk about the hurt. I grieved in a peculiar, damaging way. I coped with my father-in-law's death the same way I did with my father's; I drowned myself in work, and I continued to drink heavily. The work used to take my mind off the family matters, and the drinks would numb my soul. His death was a bombshell, and that is what sent me over the edge. I tried to grieve, but I did not know how to, so I just grew more and more distant from everyone around me, including my family. This was when Alicia and I started having troubles, and we only stayed married for a few years after that.

Acceptance did not come easily to me when either of my fathers died. If I have to put a finger, it was when I became a minister that I was able to address things that I could not back then. Since there is no set length of time for grief, you can't advise someone to get over something more quickly if you grieve faster. For some people, it happens quickly; for some, it takes time; and for some, the acceptance might never come. The important thing is to understand and address the issue and ask for help.

My father-in-law was an ideal man with a big heart who was always there for other people, which is why I celebrate him as the hero he was. In His Cross Never Burns, a book my mother-in-law wrote about Dad George's life, she wrote about his courageous nature and valor. I always saw him in a heroic light, as if he were a man like Martin Luther King and Jesse Jackson. He had a stalwart nature and steadfast personality, which is attributed to his having a lot to his name. During the Civil Rights Movement, he played an active part in Florida. There, he was a community and civil rights activist, which got him bomb threats, and he had to move. He also pastored churches in South Carolina, Fort Lauderdale, and Florida. Even in Pittsburgh, he served as a pastor at Grace Memorial for 20 years. All his life, he fulfilled his duties as a human being to the fullest. He was always there for people and helped them with their needs. I could not commemorate him as the man of God that he truly was during his lifetime because I had not yet discovered my calling. But now that I've gone down a similar path, I praise Dad George's existence every time I think of God. Only with time do we mature and realize the things that have gone by. I often think about what relationship he and I would share if Dad George were to see me now, as a minister, on the path of God. As I mentioned, he was not judgmental and never once frowned upon my lifestyle back then.

But time truly is the greatest teacher. He had seen something in me that I, myself, was unable to see back then. His keen and observant way of viewing life, though, enlightened him with a pearl of unmatched wisdom. Whenever I look at my son, Sy, who is a professional football player, I think he has my dad's and Dad George's spirit in him. Only through recollections of the beautiful time I have spent with him can I honor his memories. During his life, I knew how blessed I was to know him, but after his death, the realization truly hit me: what a phenomenon Reverend Samuel Williams George was, and I had the privilege and honor of knowing him.

# Chapter 8: New Beginnings

In life, it is not necessary that every new beginning comes with just glad tidings. Sometimes, there are memories of the past that are still lodged deep within your life and that you must pick up by yourself. Don't be afraid of them. It might be painful to pluck them out, but carrying them forward with you is even more painful.

Before I got divorced in September 2014, my former wife Alicia and I were separated for six months. It was a tough period in life. I did not know what to make of my life and what it had become, but I was never someone who would let the weight on their shoulders stop them from moving forward.

Emotionally, I was in a terrible state and place; my long-time partner and I had decided to separate ways after having two children together. Decisions like these are never easy. Divorces are never easy, not just for the two people directly involved but for everyone connected to them.

Even before my divorce, I had left Columbus, Ohio, and moved to Denver. I had to get away from everything. It was a difficult decision, but I made it nonetheless. Sometimes, it is these decisions that seem impossible at the moment that lead to different, new doors in life. You must always look out for what's out there waiting for you and provide yourself with room to grow and explore.

When I left in June, I was full of regrets. My son was very young, and he needed his father. He was only in eighth grade, whereas my daughter Sammie was going to Columbia University in Chicago. However, there was an opportunity waiting for me in Denver. I was offered a high-profile position as the first corporate security director in the cannabis industry. The position was like history-making for me.

This once-in-a-lifetime opportunity came to me from Tripp Keeber when he called and asked me if I would be interested in the job. He was the CEO of the company, Dixie Brands, at the time, but Tripp and I went way back. We worked together in 2000 and 2001. Back then, he worked for a dot com company, and they were doing a lot of closures. I was appointed as his protection agent. From there on, we had come a long way.

In September, I flew back to Ohio to continue with the divorce proceedings. My headspace was completely wrecked at that point, and I had no idea what I was doing. I just knew I had to get away from the situation. I went to the court without an attorney, and it hit me like a truck. It left me in a terrible condition; I was completely destroyed financially.

I did not know which way to turn to or whom to call out. Back then, I was not very religious, so I wholly submerged myself in drinking and working. My coping mechanisms kept me afloat until they no longer could when I put a gun in my mouth. It was then that I reevaluated my life completely.

However, things don't turn around overnight. There are long phases in life that you have to spend just keeping yourself afloat, going where the waves take you. The divorce had a major impact on me financially. I was down low, but the toll that it took on my mental and physical health was incomparable. My new job came with a lot of responsibilities, and in a way that turned out in my favor, during the harshest of times, I could completely lose myself in work, and for extensively long hours, I would not know where the time went. However, the nights were the hardest. I was alone; I had no one at that time – not even God. I used to cry endlessly and experience emotional breakdowns every other day.

Life is hard, but you must always remember that there is light at the end of the tunnel. We make mistakes, learn from them, and try to become better people. As long as people ascribe to this idea, they do get to see the nascent sun. You must know that nobody can change the past; it is the future that we can work towards.

As the director of corporate security, I had a crucial role in protecting all the employees and all the assets in the facility. Occupying such a vital position, I could not bring my personal problems to work, so I worked all those long hours with a brave face and persevered through. I did not want anyone around me to know just how deep into depression I was.

It is never easy to incorporate sense and awareness into people, but as the director of corporate security, it was a job just that. Not only did I have to make security plans, but I also had to create a secure environment where all the employees were conscious about security. I had to build a corporate culture and mindset where security was prioritized by everyone in the same way.

It was a gigantic responsibility, and I knew that it was a tightrope. I had to be mentally present to work on these big ideas because a lot was at stake, and I would have to be held accountable for it. Even though Tripp and I had a very strong, unshakable relationship, I still had a crucial task to perform: get the employees to buy into the security program, and a lot depended on me.

I was introduced to Dixie Brands, with a lot of bells and whistles and a very solid background. I had a resume that was chock full of accomplishments; I worked several Olympic games, the World Bank, and IMF meetings in Washington D.C. Then the military experience and my activation after 9/11. With this much experience under my belt, I could not let the downs get the better of me.

However, that is not to say that I could put up a brave face all the time. When dealing with the employees and colleagues, I miraculously put everything at bay and focused on the urgent tasks at hand, but when I left that facility and found myself alone in my room, I would crumble completely. There were instances when I looked in the mirror and did not recognize myself – *I did not know who I was*.

In life, there are places where we find ourselves lost, looking for an anchor or something that would help us identify who we are because everything that constitutes us is inevitably lost. I had a family, a wife, children, and a home, but I did not. It was extremely painful to redefine myself and let go of the past, but one must do it, so I did.

In 2014, there was severe attention being paid to the cannabis industry in the state of Colorado as marijuana was legalized. My experience of the job was that there was a lot of media coverage. At my facility alone, they had CBS News, CNN,

ABC News, and many other media outlets interviewing our CEO, Tripp, and Chief Operating Officer, Chuck Smith. When I first got there, they were filming a program on CNBC called Pot Barons of Colorado, which featured all these executives who were getting into the cannabis industry, and Tripp, my CEO, was a part of it. There were cameras all over the facility, even though, at that time, I did not want to be on camera. It was a new experience, and I have always believed that you must open yourself to new experiences and opportunities, so I ended up being a part of it.

I relished the job, and my relationship with the employees there was strong. We held mutual respect and trust for each other, and as all the employees there were young, my office was a safe space for them if they had any sort of problems. I was a big brother or father to many of them, and they trusted me with their problems.

So, in a way, I was ministering even before I was an ordained minister. Mentoring is much like ministering except for the references drawn from the Biblical scriptures. The employees would come and get stuff off their chests, and I would provide a safe space where nothing would ever go out of these doors, so they often came and used it.

My job at Dixie Brands was two of the best years professionally. I immensely enjoyed the work and the environment. It was a high-profile position, with no pun intended, and it came with its perks. I knew Governor Hickenlooper by first name, and we would all be invited to his house for Christmas parties. Similarly, Mayor Michael Hancock of Denver also knew me by my first name. The job was high profile because my CEO, Tripp, enjoyed a very reputable position. He was always all over the news and media, and all eyes were centered on him in the cannabis industry in Denver. But life is never simply black or white. It is always somewhere in the middle, in the gray area that you will find yourself in. For me, even though I was thriving professionally, in my personal space, I was going through one of the worst times. I was struggling, and the dilemma for me was how to cope.

I was terrified of the idea of letting anybody know, and it was exhausting to keep everyone away and at a distance. This is one of the main problems with people who are depressed quietly. They try to hide away from the world and make sure that nobody finds out about them or their mental conditions. This constant struggle then continues to exhaust them and make them feel even more alienated.

When I look back at the pictures from those times, all I see is a skeleton. My physical health had extremely deteriorated. I was just skin and bones. I was down to 170 pounds, and that is the lightest I have ever been. My jackets and suits used to hang off of me.

I used to work for probably 70 hours a week, Monday through Saturday, and even after that, some on Sundays, I would go in and catch up on the email. I would continuously work for long stretches to distract myself from my own thoughts. Working on five to eight months to even year-long assignments had become the norm for me.

Working long hours and drinking were my escape mechanisms. In retrospect, I realize how I should have tried other channels and coped with the turmoil in a different way, but back then, I was completely alone, and I had to survive in whatever way I could. My divorce had been turbulent for the family, the kids especially, and all of these realizations just made it harder and harder to get through the days. I cannot speak about the headspace that my former wife was in with certainty and convection, but mine was completely distraught.

Even then, I used to fly out to Pennsylvania because my former wife, Alicia, and my son, Sy, were living in Pittsburgh, my hometown, where they had moved from Columbus, Ohio. I used to go to see my son play football, and even though it was 1500 miles apart, I tried to get as involved as I could. He was in ninth grade back then and used to play for the junior team. It was a blessing for me that I used to watch him play.

But living with a family torn apart because of circumstances is hard. I used to miss my children and what I had back then. It is not easy to part ways with your loved ones and find yourself hit rock bottom and then do it all alone. It is just plain torture.

Back then, I did not even have God and his supreme will to hold on to because my faith was not strong. I did not go to church regularly. In all of my time in Denver, I have gone to church once or twice, maybe. With a non-existent faith and raging depression, I was bound to wind up where I did on 18th April 2015, with a gun in my mouth, about to end it all.

# Chapter 9: Mental Health Crisis

There are days like the 18th of April 2015 that could change the course of one's life. For me, depression was something that haunted me in the dark of night. In the days, it remained in the shadows, peering at me from between the spaces but never confronting me out in the open.

My days remained busy, and I was extremely invested professionally. I did not let my mental health issues bleed over into my daily job. It was a high-profile job, and I knew the risks. Although the job was stressful, I simply relished it as I was the first-ever Director of Corporate Security in the cannabis sector.

The mornings were filled with extensive tasks and media appearances. I got to have interviews with the New York Times and even with Security 500 magazine. I was continuously involved with my fellow employees and law enforcement as the FBI wanted to know more about the cannabis industry.

But the nights, alone at home with no company but my own, that is when I struggled. It was the difficult part. There were no activities I could or was engaging myself in at that point. I was not even working out; I was just skin and bones. Although, for some people, I was not in bad shape, yet for me, considering that I had been a professional wrestler, it really hit me hard not being in good shape.

Slowly, the thoughts kept piling up: the stress of leaving wrestling prematurely, the stress of the divorce and the heartbreak that followed, leaving my children and family behind, and being in Denver, 1500 miles away from everyone. I could not stop myself from spiraling every single night. My routine was drinking heavily at night and then putting up a brave face in the morning at work. But how long could this have worked? And, so, it led to the fateful day of the 18th of April.

I had planned to end my life for months on end and even looked at different potential places because I could not do it in my own room. My roommate at the time had a roommate who took his life, and I did not want to put him through it. I could not bring myself to be the cause of his reliving the trauma, and so I contemplated renting a hotel room.

However, and it may be selfish, I eventually decided to end it all in my office. Then, I did not know why I had made this decision. Still, looking back now, I realize how traumatic it would have been for everyone there if I had gone with my plan. So, I want to apologize to everyone at Dixie. I am sorry for ever thinking of something that would have affected you all majorly.

In the early months of 2015, I finally decided it was time. I was not afraid at all; I was just confused about where and how I would do it. I thought about how it would affect everyone and the precipitating events. But the weight of everything that had happened, from my wrestling career to losing both of my dads and then getting divorced and being financially devastated, all of it was too heavy and clouded my judgment.

I could no longer function, so I said to myself, "Okay. I cannot do this anymore. I just simply can't do it, and I'd be better off dead." I thought I would be better off if I was no longer here, and that is what I worked toward. It happened on a Saturday, and I walked into the office like any other day. Usually, when I mingled with everyone in the office, I would put on a chef's smock and a hat and go into the kitchen. We used to manufacture cannabisinfused chocolates, and I would go in and try to make chocolates with everyone.

Of course, when it came to cooking, I was not a professional, so the chocolates never turned out well. Then, the staff would playfully kick me out and tell me I was best at protection and was not needed in the kitchen. All of this was done in fun and games as we were all very friendly and comfortable with each other. We would all laugh as I would give them a hard time.

Similarly, I also wanted Saturday to be as normal as possible. I did not want any employees to think something was wrong with me. So, I walked around and did everything as I did every Saturday. I ensured that they knew that I was there to support them and in case someone wanted to come and talk to me in my office.

Although I made everything seem normal on the surface, deep within, nothing was okay because that day would mark the last day of my life on this earth. And when everybody cleared out and I told every last employee goodbye, I ensured the facility was secure and went to my office.

My office was the most secure place in the entire facility. I had cameras everywhere, and not a single leaf could fall, which I would not have known about. Alone in my office, I pulled out like a gallon of top-notch vodka. But, suddenly, looking at the bottle, I realized that I wouldn't drink it. I did not need the liquor to help me get through this; I was courageous enough to take the step all on my own. I rarely ever had a round in the chamber, unlike other law enforcement officers who always had a round on them. Even though I always had my Glock 19 on my hip like a body part, I never felt comfortable with the idea of putting in a round all the time. I only ever put one if I perceived a genuine threat and I needed to protect myself from others, which only happened twice in my career.

In my office, I jacked around into the chamber, then I leaned back and put the gun in my mouth. Everything was static for a moment; although the music was music, you could hear the light hum of all the cameras working and the HVAC system. Slowly, I put the pressure on the trigger, marking it as my last act, and after that, everything went dark.

***

In that darkness, I initially thought that I had done it, that I had pulled the trigger. I was surprised that I did not feel a single thing. I tried to understand my situation and surroundings and thought that maybe this was the first stage of death. But everything was completely still and silent – no lights, music, or cameras- and then I felt it. It was an odd sensation that crawled down my spine. I felt the hair on my arms rise, and some sort of electrical charge went through me.

The spiritual experience is quite difficult to put into words, but it almost felt like being struck by lightning. Once, as a kid, I played baseball with my friends, and lightning struck the outfield fence. Everybody had felt an electrical charge. Fortunately for us, nobody had been struck. But, at that moment, dangling between life and death, I felt that charge again, and I believe it was God's way of telling me that He is with me. I was utterly nervous and couldn't feel anything, but there was a strong sense of someone's presence. I don't know how best to explain it, but I felt that I was not alone that there were two individuals with me there. And, even though I could not see them, I could smell them; their familiar scent greeted me from every which way.

The familiar wafts of air made me realize that I was not alone there; my dad and my father-in-law, Dad George, were there in that space, somewhere between life and death. Although their presence escaped my naked eye, I could feel their individual selves all around me.

A low murmur of voices continuously fell into my ears. In that blurry haste, all I could make out was that my dad was kneeling on my left side. And I could feel a strong, familiar hand on my right shoulder; it was my father-in-law.

All I could make out of the low murmurs was that my dad was quite upset while dad George was trying to diffuse the situation. I heard his voice; he said, "Son, do you realize what you're going to leave in your wake?"

As soon as he said those words, an old projector screen appeared in front of me, and my whole life flashed before my eyes. I could hear the reels as they displayed my life: my kids being born, my career in the military, my time as a professional wrestler, losing my family members, and every other emotional moment. I watched everything, but just when I hoped that it would be over, it showed me in the office – taking my own life.

I watched as I shot myself, the blood splattered everywhere. It was up against the wall, and I watched as my body slumped over. The blood dripped down on the cabinets of my office, and both my father and father-in-law asked if this was what I really wanted. I could barely get the words out, but I said no. I did not want this; being a spectator to my own death was an experience that I would never be able to comprehend myself. It was an otherworldly experience, and it will always stay with me.

As soon as I said no, the lights came on in the room, the 80 cameras in the room came to life one by one, and then the music started playing. It was a song that I will never forget. I have even titled this book after the song Out of the Storm by the band Incognito, which has a very good friend of mine, Bluey, as its band leader.

That night, I returned to my condo in Denver and sat there completely perplexed. I did not know how to comprehend what had just happened. I kept raking my brain, thinking if I was tripping, but I had not taken drugs or alcohol that day, and I was not even exhausted. So, it could not have been a dream or hallucination I had experienced either.

I carried this incident with me for five years. I did not know how to understand it; I did not even know how to express it and who to express it to. I just figured that it would be better if I had just forgotten about it. Put this away and never revisit it.

At that time, I did not realize it was a divine intervention; I just thought it was something peculiar and could not give a proper name. And, because I was unable to understand it myself, I hesitated to share it with anybody. I feared that people would think that I was just crazy. The whole phenomenon was unexplainable. I did not see my dad or my father-in-law, but their scent made me realize who I was within that state. You tend to recognize the voices and smells of the people you are around, which indicates their presence to me then as well. Although I could not see them, I knew they were there trying to help me, and that help was God-sent.

At the time, the meaning behind it was lost on me, but when I stopped drinking in the Pacific Northwest, God finally revealed himself to me, and only then I understood everything. It was 2020; five years had passed when I could read the miracle for what it was. I didn't immediately turn to God, which people might find odd, but everybody has time when they return to the Lord.

Even though I did not have a complete change of heart, I did walk away with something, completely and utterly sure — I was never going to try to take my life again.

# Chapter 10: Reinvention

The day I stopped myself from pulling the trigger was the day I knew, without a shadow of a doubt, that I would never cross that line again. The abyss stared back at me, and I had decided I didn't want to dive into it. The hard part was not over yet.

Walking away from that moment didn't mean I was suddenly all right. The darkness that had been my constant companion was still there. The depression remained! I didn't know how to clear it, but I knew I had to keep walking.

The truth is, I didn't tackle my depression after that day. I didn't have a grand plan of recovery. I simply knew I had to find a way to exist. Reinvention, as I would come to learn, isn't about transforming overnight. It's about finding a reason to keep going, even when you don't know what that reason is. It's about learning to live with the shadows without letting them consume you. I didn't tackle depression, not at first. But I took that first step away from the edge, and that's what made all the difference.

One name I can't forget in this struggle of my life was Alex Golston. Just two weeks after my suicide, a conversation with him created all the difference that was needed. But first, let me tell you how we met. This was yet another interesting tale.

When I arrived at Dixie, the corporate headquarters was still under construction. So, our offices were a couple of trailers set up on-site. It was a makeshift operation, and security was already a concern, especially after someone broke into the trailers about a week before I even got there. Given the state of things, I needed help, someone reliable, experienced, and unafraid to step into uncertain territory. That's when I was introduced to Alex. I called him while I was still on the East Coast before even stepping foot in Denver. He came highly recommended, so I reached out, and he agreed to handle the situation with the break-in. That was the first time I heard his voice, and he seemed professional, calm, and efficient.

When I finally got to Denver and met him in person, I was surprised. With a name like "Alex Golston," I wasn't expecting a large, muscular African American man who looked like he belonged on a movie set. He filled the doorway of the trailer, towering over me with a presence that was both intimidating and welcoming. His voice was deep, but he had a friendly demeanor, which put me at ease almost immediately. He seemed like a Greek God.

Alex was a former SWAT officer, and I could tell he knew what he was doing. It was a relief because the cannabis industry at that time was a cash-heavy business. Federal laws prevented us from having traditional bank accounts, so all the cash we collected had to be deposited in ATMs. It was a risky setup, and there were only two Bank of America ATMs in the entire city, with no physical branches.

This made every cash deposit a potential security risk, but Alex stepped in and took care of it for us. He and another retired Denver cop handled all our deposits, making sure everything was done safely and discreetly. It was a massive weight off my shoulders, knowing I could rely on him to handle the cash without any problems. Despite his size and strength, Alex wasn't just muscle but had a brain to match. His background in SWAT gave him a unique perspective on security, and he was always a step ahead, anticipating what might go wrong and planning accordingly. This made him invaluable to me, especially in an industry where the stakes were high, and the rules were constantly changing.

Over time, Alex became more than just a security consultant. He was someone I could turn to for guidance. He was easy to talk to and had a great sense of humor, often sharing stories. He had this way of making you feel like everything would be okay, no matter how chaotic things seemed.

The relationship I built with Alex was more than just business. He was a friend, someone I could count on to have my back when things got tough. Thus, I profoundly leaned on Alex.

Thereby, two weeks after my darkest moment, my buddy Alex called. It was a simple call, nothing dramatic, just business as usual. But that call would turn out to be one of the critical moments in my drive back to life. I remember Alex was someone who you just felt to be safer around. A person who seemed like he could handle any situation that came his way. When he reached out, he had an idea that he needed help with.

"Hey, Sy, do you have any contacts in Africa?" he asked. Luckily, I did, in fact, have plenty. A good friend of mine ran a security company in South Africa, with offices all over the continent. Alex wanted some assistance in business, so I agreed to make the connection.

After I set up the introduction, Alex came back to me with a request. He said that he was going to travel to South Africa and wanted me to accompany him. He said that he thought it made more sense if I was to be there as he were to meet my friend. Indeed, it made sense that having someone familiar with the job to bridge that gap was a good idea.

So I said yes, and we booked our tickets. It was the first time in a long time that I felt a spark of excitement. But it wasn't until the wheels of our plane left the runway in Denver that I felt something shift. It was like a weight had been lifted off my chest and a sudden sense of relief that I couldn't quite explain. I was back in the air, doing what I'd always loved. Traveling!

The journey to South Africa was long from Denver to LA, then from LAX to Abu Dhabi, and then from Abu Dhabi to Johannesburg, and finally from Johannesburg to Cape Town. Alex and I had plenty of time to talk along the way. We discussed business, life, and everything in between. He knew I'd been through a lot due to my job stress and my divorce. However, he didn't know the full extent of what I'd been battling. I hadn't told him about the suicide attempt, and I had no plan to.

But Alex knew that something was terribly off. During our conversation during this whole tour, he turned to me and said, "Sy, I know you're a professional wrestler. I've seen some of your pictures. You should get back into the gym." It wasn't a heavyhanded suggestion but just a casual comment. But it struck a chord.

Alex was a big guy, about 6'5" and 250 pounds, with a solid wall of muscle. He was an avid lifter and had that physique that made you think twice before crossing him. His suggestion came from a good place. From a friend who cared and wanted to help. He didn't know I was battling depression, but he knew I was struggling. Getting back into the gym seemed like a simple, tangible step I could take. The more he talked about it, the more I realized he was right. I needed something to focus on, something to pull me out of the gloominess. The idea of getting back into the gym, getting back into shape, and building strength felt like a lifeline. It wasn't just about getting physically fit, but it was about finding a way to start healing. To start feeling like myself again. Therefore, it was a mental upliftment as well.

When we finally landed in Cape Town, I was already thinking about how I could make this work. And so, the trip to Cape Town was more than just a business trip. It was the beginning of a new chapter. A turning point that I desperately needed. It was Alex's simple suggestion, his encouragement, that planted the seed of hope. Getting back into the gym became my way of regaining control and finding a path forward. Slowly but surely, it began to work. Physically, I started to feel stronger. Mentally, I began to see myself in the mirror again as the person I used to be.

Alex may not have realized it at the time, but his suggestion to get back into the gym was the first step toward my healing. I really credit him with my physical transformation. He was instrumental in guiding me back into fitness, suggesting which gym I should check out in Aurora, Colorado.

The gym was a place where I could start rebuilding my bodily strength while slowly working on my mental health. Even though I knew that finding a gym wouldn't magically fix my depression, it was a step in the right direction. I carried that burden for another five years, but at least I had something positive to focus on. Alex didn't just help me with the physical side of things. He was there for me on a personal level, too. We'd go out for beers and talk about everything from work to life in general. Those nights were a relief and a chance to let loose and have some fun. Alex had a way of making things seem less daunting, even when my job at Dixie was anything but easy.

At Dixie, I was the director of corporate security, which meant I was responsible for everything from safeguarding the premises to handling the cash flow. The cannabis industry was booming, but it came with its own set of challenges. Alex was a massive help in that regard. He not only took care of the cash deposits but also advised me on security measures.

I was a one-man shop, trying to keep everything together at Dixie, and Alex's support was invaluable. He stepped in where I needed him, whether it was handling money or setting up security systems.

Looking back, I realize how crucial Alex was during that time. He was more than a consultant. He was a partner, someone I could rely on without question. He gave me the push I needed to get back, which started me on a journey of physical and mental recovery.

Alex might downplay his role, saying I did all the work myself, but he was the catalyst for change. He planted the seeds of hope and encouraged me to keep moving forward. Without him, I don't know if I would have found the strength to continue.

***

I continued to work at Dexter Branch for another year. Then, I decided it was time for a change. I moved from downtown Denver out to Aurora, Colorado, where I found Colorado Pro

Gym. It was a big place filled with bodybuilders, weightlifters, and powerlifters, all throwing around iron. The atmosphere was welcoming, and I felt at home from the moment I walked in. The people there were genuine, and even though I wasn't a regular yet, I could tell they appreciated everyone.

It was a slow process of rebuilding myself. The depression didn't just disappear because I found a new gym or moved to a new town. Nevertheless, I kept working on myself, trying to make the best of each day. But it wasn't until I stopped drinking on March 1st, 2020, that I began to truly embrace change. It took five years for me to reach that point. Five years of struggling, of trying to piece myself together bit by bit. And yet, despite all the ups and downs, there was one constant that I never thought about suicide again.

That was the biggest takeaway from that day when I walked out of my office, never looking back. I didn't realize it at the time, but it was a spiritual encounter. I wasn't religious, and I didn't have enough faith back then to understand that God might have intervened on my behalf. It wasn't until much later, after I quit drinking and started reevaluating my life, that I saw the truth of what had happened. But even then, I didn't want to explore it. I wanted to bury that memory so deep in my soul that I wouldn't have to think about it again.

But God has a way of reaching you, even when you're not looking for Him. When I stopped drinking in 2020, it was like everything I'd tried to bury came bubbling up to the surface. It forced me to confront the spiritual aspect of my encounter, to finally accept that something beyond my understanding had taken place. I wasn't ready to explore it fully, but I knew I couldn't ignore it anymore. It was frustrating not being able to explain what had happened. I was analytical by nature, always trying to think things through, and this was something I couldn't wrap my mind around. But maybe that was the point. Maybe I needed to stop trying to control everything and let go. Perhaps it was nature's way of telling me to trust that things would work out. It was a hard lesson, but it was one I needed to learn.

# Chapter 11: Olympics (2016)

My adventures in the Olympics weren't as twisted or difficult. I'd worked several Olympics before I worked in Beijing in 2008. I provided threat assessments and intelligence reports for many events. These included intel reports for Sydney in 2000 and Athens in 2004. However, my security industry experience was another reason for my going to the Olympics in 2016. My reputation in the security industry was solid. It was built on years of experience and a flair for handling high-pressure situations. And so, I was off to the Olympics.

Stepping down from my passion to being in the Olympics was an easy task. Despite my love for Dixie and the work we were doing, I knew it was time for a change. So, after my second year, I made the difficult decision to step down from my position. It was challenging in the sense that I had poured myself soulfully into the company. Building a team and shaping the security protocols that would keep the company safe was all I did for a considerable time.

I had already decided to leave Dixie if I hadn't even worked at the Olympics. After agreeing to work as the director of corporate security for Dixie Brands for a year or two, I quit during the second year already.

Considering the time I spent at Dixie, I could not say bye without arranging for an alternative. I had faith in the team I'd built. But someone needed to fill my shoes. Thus, I had hired my replacement, Colin Daugherty. I was comfortable leaving that position in his hands. Just two days after leaving Dixie, I received a call that would change everything. Two days after I resigned from Dixie Brands, and as I was relaxing poolside at my condo in Aurora, I got a call out of the blue from a D.C.-based Security Firm. It was a company in Washington asking if I could respond quickly to a situation in Rio. They had a vice president who was struggling, and they needed someone with my expertise to help set things right.

They asked me if I would be able to deploy quickly to Rio de Janeiro to help out their personnel who were working at the Rio 2016 Summer Games. They said that the VP on the ground had a lot being thrown his way, and he may be in the "deep end," meaning the program was faltering. It was a daunting prospect to walk into a situation I knew nothing about. But I couldn't resist the challenge. Moreover, I had my experience at the Beijing Summer Games in China and Hong Kong in 2008. Thus, I thought that it could not be much different.

I packed my bags and boarded a plane to Rio, ready to face whatever lay ahead. It was time for me to pursue a new venture that eventually took me to the heart of the Olympic Games. As I boarded that plane to Rio, I felt both excitement and trepidation at the same time. The future was a blurry path to me, and without knowing what I was stepping into, I was ready to embrace whatever challenges came my way. I was walking into a really bad situation, and I didn't know it at the time.

Arriving in Rio, I was thrust into rapid activity. The company I was working with needed me to hit the ground running, and there was no time to waste. I met with the struggling vice president, and it quickly became clear that the situation was dire.

In spite of their best efforts, things had got out of control. They needed someone with a fresh perspective to help them get back on track. It was a challenging assignment, but I was determined to make a difference.

When I first reached Denver to take on a position in the cannabis industry, I faced skepticism and disdain from many of my colleagues in the security industry. They viewed my decision as a misstep. They thought it a move that would tarnish my reputation and brand me as "damaged goods." For a while, I felt alone in an industry that was still new to me and was stigmatized and misunderstood.

But as time went on, I began to garner positive attention for my work in the cannabis space and my personal transformation. People started to take notice of the impact I was making and reconsidered their initial judgments. Slowly but surely, I earned back their respect and proved that my decision to work in cannabis was not only a good one but a necessary one.

However, when I transitioned to working at the Olympics, I quickly realized that I had walked into a hornet's nest. Even though it was a big deal considering it was for the Olympics, which is undoubtedly the second most watched sport after the World Cup, and it was like a wheelhouse for me, I was under a burden. The company that hired me had failed to inform me of the problems brewing on the ground in Rio, leaving me unprepared for the magnitude of the situation. The executive I was brought in to help had alienated himself from the locals and made enemies along the way. His lack of respect for the Brazilian culture had caused severe damage to the company's reputation and relationships in the community. It was a delicate situation, and I knew that I had my work cut out for me. I couldn't help but feel frustrated by the lack of preparation on the company's part as I dove into the task of repairing the damage and rebuilding trust with the locals. They had put me in a difficult position, expecting me to clean up a mess that I had not been adequately briefed on.

Yet, drawing on my strengths in relationship-building and diplomacy, I worked tirelessly to mend fences. I tried to restore the company's standing in Rio. It was an unnerving task, and I did everything I could to handle the situation. While I may not have been able to undo all the damage that had been done, I took solace in knowing that I had done everything in my power to make amends and set things right. However, in the middle of the restlessness of my work and the thrill of being in Rio, there was a struggle with alcohol that I couldn't rid myself of. Though I had tried my best to leave behind thoughts of suicide, I found solace in drinking. This habit that had been with me for years became particularly heavy during my time in Denver and the Pacific Northwest.

Even as I hit the gym and worked on improving my physical health, the drinking persisted. It was a crutch that I leaned on every day. It was a way to numb the pain and drown out the noise of my thoughts. But instead of easing the burden, it only served to amplify my struggles. It took a toll on my joints and my overall well-being. For people who could not see it, I was still working, hanging out with friends, and enjoying the joy that life brings. Nevertheless, my inner heart was drowned in the pool of alcohol.

And consequently, the drinking part never really subsided. It continued to amplify until 2020.

*****

As I wandered the streets of Rio, soaking in the sights and sounds of the vibrant city, I stumbled upon a gym near my condo in Copacabana Beach. It was a stroke of serendipity that I found this hidden gem in a lively city like this. I was walking around, and I just happened to find this gym! I can't remember the name of it, but it was a no-frills establishment. Its blue-collar atmosphere signified that it was not for the very far away from the fancy rendezvous of the place.

Stepping inside, I was greeted by the sight of hardcore bodybuilders pumping iron and sweating it out in this space. Their devotion was palpable, and I couldn't help but feel an admiration for their commitment to their craft. As I made my way through the gym, the regulars eyed me with curiosity. They wondered who this foreigner was wandering among them. Some speculated that I might be an American celebrity visiting Rio for the Olympics, drawn to the city's allure and exhilaration. But I quickly dispelled their misconceptions. It was hard for me to converse with them, as neither their English nor my Portuguese was proficient! So we made hand and physical gestures to communicate.

However, I quickly found common ground with the locals through my clients. They always provided me with tickets to various events, and I decided to share the wealth with my newfound gym companions. Thus, I began to hand out tickets as a daily ritual, and soon I was a familiar face. I was welcomed with open arms by the tight-knit community of bodybuilders. They even initially tried to hand me some money in exchange for the tickets. Nonetheless, my intention was only to befriend them. Thus, I explained to them that it was only a symbol of extending my hand in friendship. Subsequently, I became quite amiable with some of the bodybuilders, and they also took an interest in me. We tried our best to converse, but it was difficult due to the language barrier. But I remember there was maybe one person in that gym who could speak broken English. He served as a kind of translator. It was through him that I clarified that I was no celebrity but just down there working in the Olympics.

After all of this elucidation and my gesture of handing over my tickets for free, the gym members began to trust me. I, in fact, became quite a famous gentleman in that manner. They even liked the fact that I was in excellent shape. I mean, it is not surprising they found me to be handsome, considering they thought of me as an actor at first. I am kidding, of course. It was with utter gratitude that I took their compliment. They didn't truly believe me until I told them that I was, in fact, living in a condo directly on Copacabana Beach and that the gym was only a block or two away from my condo.

As I immersed myself in the brio of Rio, I dedicated myself to my workouts at the gym on Copacabana Beach. I began to undergo a remarkable physical transformation. The commitment I made to myself and my fitness goals was firm, and it wasn't long before the results started to show.

One day, during another walk of mine in the streets of Rio, I crossed paths with a colleague from a security company I had previously consulted in Washington, DC. His surprise was evident as he exclaimed, "Sy! Sy!" He had almost failed to recognize me with so significant of a change in my appearance. The shock in his voice was clear. I had indeed shed some weight and gained muscle mass. Reconciling with my friend was refreshing. He began by telling me how different I looked, which I did. Consequently, we had a great conversation. He was down there because they had a footprint at the Olympics as well. There were plenty of companies from the US that worked down there because of the clients. Companies like McDonald's and AMEX and other corporate folks that we were advertising for the Olympics. Therefore, there were plenty of American security executives down there working, including us.

Thanks to my rigorous exercises and devotion to my physical well-being, I was back in form. I was proud of the progress I had made. My colleague's reaction was not uncommon. Many friends and acquaintances who hadn't seen me in years were taken aback by my transformation. They marveled at how different I looked and how much healthier and more vibrant I appeared.

But for me, the physical transformation went beyond mere aesthetics. It was about reclaiming control over my body and my health. It was also about feeling strong and confident in my own skin. As I continued to push myself in the gym, I could feel my self-esteem growing with each passing day. Of course, the process was not without its pains. It was during my intense training sessions in Rio that I suffered a shoulder injury, blowing out my rotator cuff. It was a setback, for sure, but soon, I was up and about, ready to be in the physical realm. Even before healing, I remained committed to my workouts. I adapted my routine to accommodate my healing shoulder. I even ran into a few friends who were shocked by my size when I went to the Olympics. I would get nice comments from them like, "Man, Oh! You look fantastic. Thus, keep doing whatever you're doing. That's how a tiny gym in Rio permanently changed my life.

# Chapter 12: The Fresh Prince of Puyallup

I had no plans for the Pacific Northwest or anywhere else for that matter when I returned from Brazil at the end of the Olympics in late August. My initial plan after leaving Dixie Brands was to become a speaker and share my insights from working in the cannabis industry. But before I could start with that new project, I was asked to join in for a much-needed vacation that came my way.

My friend Ed Elinan and his family extended an invitation for me to join them on a trip to Peru. The idea of getting away and spending some time with close friends was exactly what I needed after the intensity of my work.

Also, my first post-divorce relationship occurred in Denver. She was a phenomenal woman, although much younger than me. We dated for about six months, and she simply vanished from my life. We met in early 2016 when I moved from Denver to nearby Aurora, Colorado, which is a close suburb of Denver. She was a bartender from one of my local haunts in the Denver area and was a workout nut like me. That's probably why we were mutually attracted to one another, but I guess it was not meant to be. I certainly wish her well wherever she is! So, with anticipation, I agreed to join the Elinans.

After a few months of relaxing and regrouping in Denver, I found myself boarding a plane to Peru just after Christmas. Ed and I had worked together for years. Ever since the mid-90s, he has become more like family to me. He had been inviting me to join him and his family in Peru for years. Each time, I would agree but never quite make the trip. Finally, after years of saying yes and never going, I decided to follow through. I flew down to Peru to spend time with them. I was eager for a break and some relaxation. The flight landed in Lima, and from there, I made my way south to a serene beach location. The drive south of Lima took about an hour, and I was soon at their family compound. The place was truly sublime. This was my first real vacation in several years. I needed it more than I realized.

The Elinan family was quite welcoming and hospitable. Ed and his family were the perfect hosts. His wife, Karen, and his son, David Maximillian Elinan, welcomed me with open arms. It was a refreshing change from the high-pressure stress of the work I had been through. They made sure I felt at home and included in their activities. We used to have meals together and tell our personal stories. All in all, we simply enjoyed each other's company without any hesitance or formalities. David, whom I had watched grow up, called me "tío," which means uncle in Spanish. I rejoiced to see him again and to spend time with him and the rest of the family. They had a beautiful setup, and the beach was just a short walk away.

The calmness of the beach allowed me to think deeply about the ups and downs of my life. Even the trials I had faced and the transformations I had undergone were always in my thoughts. All of this played through my mind like a movie or a film. The physical and mental shifts I had experienced were significant. There could be nothing better than the sound of the ocean waves.

Moreover, the sinking sand that hugged warmly around my feet and the easy company of good friends provided me a respite.

It was a time of reflection and healing. I got a chance to catch my breath and think about what lay ahead. It was relaxing as well as fun. I spent my days soaking up the sun on the beach and enjoying the warm weather.

One of the most memorable moments was New Year's Eve. The Elinans hosted a fantastic party right on the beach. They had a beautiful structure built specifically for such gatherings, and we danced, ate, and celebrated well into the early hours of January 1st, 2017. Spending New Year's Eve and the first week of January 2017 on the beaches of Peru was like therapy for my soul after that suicide attempt and days of depression.

That night was particularly special. Surrounded by all this joy and laughter, I felt contentment. It was a massive contrast to the turmoil and stress I had experienced in the past few years.

By the end of it, I got so much sun that I ended up getting sunburned. This was something that didn't happen to me often. They teased me about it, saying, "The sun's got you good!" On my last day there, Ed said to me, "You go get it." He said this particularly because it was a Sunday and, of course, my last day. Before I flew back to Denver, I looked in the mirror and saw that my skin was peeling. And I was actually peeling like an orange. But the juice was worth the squeeze.

When I got back to Denver in January of 2017, I was in a state of flux. I was trying to figure out my next move. I spent some time relaxing, still riding the high of my vacation in Peru, when my good friend Bryan called me. Bryan had an offer for me that would soon change my plans. He said, "Hey, Sy, I've got a protection detail coming up. Would you be interested in helping us out as the team leader and managing the detail in Portland?" Without much reluctance, I agreed. I needed something to focus on, something to get me moving forward again. So, I packed up and flew to Portland in January of 2017 to take on this new role. The detail was intense, but I enjoyed it. It was what I knew best, and it was good to be back in the protection business.

We worked with some big clients, and the details went well. It felt good to be part of a team again. The work kept me busy and distracted, which was exactly what I needed at the time. I stayed in Portland, working on this detail until it ended in May of 2017.

Just as I was preparing to head back to Denver, Bryan approached me with an offer. He asked if I would consider coming up to the Seattle area to help him and his wife, Katherine Fath, who also goes by Dr. Katherine Martin, manage their business. My relationship had just ended, and as you already know, it left me feeling hurt and shattered.

This crack was something I needed to fill, and so if it hadn't ended, I might have stayed in Denver. However, I needed to get away. Thus, I agreed to Bryan's offer and relocated to Washington. It was a fresh start in many ways. Working with Bryan gave me a sense of purpose and stability during a turbulent time in my life.

Things started off on a high note when I relocated to Washington to work with Bryan. We were doing well in the cannabis sector with multiple clients. Our main clients were in Tacoma, Washington, where we provided security for several cannabis facilities. These facilities were involved in everything from manufacturing cannabis products to cultivating the marijuana plants themselves. Our business was flourishing, and we were making a significant impact on the security of these operations.

However, things took a turn when our biggest client had to restructure their finances. This restructuring meant they could no longer afford our services at their three main facilities. This was a huge blow to us because they were our largest source of revenue. The loss of this client had a domino effect on our business. We had to let several employees go because we simply didn't have enough work to keep them employed.

Letting people go is never easy. It was a painful process for both Bryan and me. These were people we had worked closely with, and they had become part of our team and our daily lives. It was tough to look them in the eyes and tell them we didn't have work for them anymore. It wasn't just about the business. It was about the personal connections we had made and the responsibility we felt towards our employees. It hurt to see them go. It was a picturization of the volatility of the industry we were in.

The loss of our biggest client was a significant hit to our company. It didn't just affect the finances but also affected the morale of the team. We had been riding high on the success of our work, and this setback felt like a punch to the gut. We had worked so hard to build those relationships and to provide highquality security services. Seeing it all slip away was devastating!

Personally, this period was particularly challenging for me. I was already dealing with the emotional fallout from my recent breakup and my suicide attempt and depression. This professional setback only added to my feelings of hurt and despair. It felt like I couldn't catch a break. I tried to bring more business on board to compensate for the loss, but it was an uphill battle. The stress and pressure were immense. Not too surprisingly, it took a toll on my mental health.

It's very gray and rainy in Seattle in the winter. It gets dark early. This just made the situation worse for me. Bryan was very positive and said, "Hey, we can keep going. We can keep doing this." I was despondent. I did manage to say, "Yeah, let's keep pushing. Let's keep pushing." But deep down, I knew that losing that big client was a big hit for both of us. We were getting by, but it wasn't the revenue we were accustomed to. If I am honest, we were pinching pennies.

My drinking, which was already substantial, got even worse after this. The company was hurting, and so was I. The lack of natural light of nature and the constant rain were adding to my troubles. The aura of melancholy was enough to make me feel more dejected. And then the financial stress! All this contributed to my growing depression. Each day felt heavier than the last, and I found it increasingly hard to stay motivated. The gray skies outside seemed to seep into my mind. They clouded my thoughts and dampened my spirit.

Bryan still tried to stay optimistic. He always encouraged us. However, on the other hand, I couldn't let go of the feeling of despair. The pressure of keeping the business afloat, combined with my personal struggles, felt overwhelming. Nights were the hardest. I would sit alone with a bottle of drink in hand and try to drown out the noise in my head. The alcohol was a temporary escape, but it never really helped. It just numbed the pain for a while, only for it to return with a gloominess the next day. As I mentioned earlier, we had to let several people go. And this was undoubtedly the most difficult. Telling someone they no longer had a job, even though you know they relied on that income, could be gut-wrenching. It added to my sense of failure and hopelessness. The constant stress and anxiety started to affect my health. I wasn't sleeping well, and my body felt like it was running on empty. The endless gray days in Seattle seemed to stretch on forever. The future felt as bleak as the Seattle winter. I was stuck in a cycle of despair that I couldn't break free from.

There were moments when I would look out at the rainsoaked streets and wonder how things had gone so wrong. The sense of loss, both personally and professionally, was crushing. I felt disconnected from everything and everyone, including myself. The struggle to keep going and to keep pushing was now like a losing battle. Every day was a reminder of what we had lost and how far we had fallen.

The gray, rainy winters of Seattle remained unbearable. It's been said that many people battle depression in this region due to the lack of sunlight and constant rain. I was no exception. My mental health sank deeper into hopelessness as the days grew darker and colder. While some might call it seasonal depression, for me, it was a year-round battle that only intensified in the winter months. My drinking continued unabated. The alcohol offered temporary relief, but it was never enough to fill the void inside.

During this time, I frequently visited bars and other such places. One of these was HG Bistro, which was a local haunt. I was a regular there and was known by many. The chef, the bartenders, and the waitstaff were all familiar faces. One bartender, in particular, took to calling me the "Fresh Prince of Puyallup." She used to say, "Sy, you are so dynamic," and that I looked like the iconic character from the TV series "The Fresh Prince of Bel-Air," the one in which Will Smith starred. She went about it once, "Yeah, you're like the Fresh Prince of Puyallup." Everybody thought it was a funny thing. The nickname stuck, and soon, everyone in the bar knew me as the Fresh Prince of Puyallup.

# Chapter 13: Bliss in Patience

Those days, I never missed a workout but felt isolated and yearning to be closer to family at the time. It was tough, although I was staying with very good friends, whom I now consider family. I still felt isolated because the Pacific Northwest is so far removed from where any of my family members were. Nobody was even close to being up in the Pacific Northwest. The feeling of separation was profound. My friends in Seattle were supportive, and I appreciated their company. However, the physical distance from my family was unbearable. Every time I would look at the calendar and realize another holiday or important event was approaching, the fear of missing out on those moments with my family became more intense.

Hence, it just felt gloomy at times. I often found myself thinking about my son and how much I wanted to be there for him, not just for his football games but for the everyday moments, too. I was hustling to go back and forth from Seattle to Pittsburgh to watch him play high school and then on to college football. So, I was flying a lot to try to be there for him. The effort to be present for his games was taxing, both financially and emotionally. With the long flights and the quick turnarounds, I was always tired. I pushed myself to make it to as many games as I could, knowing how important my presence was to him and how much I valued those moments. I couldn't make every game just because of the distance, but I did make it to a lot of his games.

It was difficult being that far away. The separation from my family also meant missing out on the little things that make life special. This seclusion brought with it sadness and longing that was hard to break.

Living in the Pacific Northwest, so far from my family, felt like being in a different world. It was a strange experience for me. The region felt so different from any place I had lived before. I was antsy up there. But I knew I was trying to help my dear friend, who I consider my brother. Bryan was like my brother, and we were very close.

Therefore, I did everything I could to make sure that the company was able to move forward. It was getting grueling, and I kept asking, why am I even up here? Out of all the places I would pick to go, why would it be the Pacific Northwest? Though I shared a strong bond with Bryan, the constant question in my mind was why I had chosen to be there. Every morning, as I woke up to the sound of rain tapping against the window, I wondered what had driven me to this corner of the country. The lack of acquainted faces, the distance from family, and the foreign environment all added to my despondence.

Now, although the summers in the Pacific Northwest offered a complete contrast to the blue winters, it's beautiful up there and probably the best place to be in the U.S. because it's not very humid. In fact, it's spectacular. The transformation was almost magical.

In the winter, it rained endlessly, which was dreary and dark. But in summer, the rain would give way to clear skies, and the entire region would come alive. The natural beauty that surrounded me during these months was breathtaking. The long days seemed to stretch endlessly, with the sun shining in the sky well into the evening. It didn't get dark till about 11 o'clock because of where we were geographically. We could sit outside, and you could still see the sunset, though the sun seemed like a giant orange.

Sitting outside with Bryan, watching the sunset paint the firmament in hues of orange and pink, provided moments of peace. It was during these times that I could simply enjoy the present. The cool breeze, greenery, and serenity of a Pacific Northwest summer were remarkable. Yet, the winters in the Pacific Northwest were still far from pulchritudinous. The days grew shorter, the skies turned gray, and the rain seemed to fall incessantly from the heavens above.

I found myself dealing with the same questions that I couldn't answer. Why had God brought me to this place at this time? What was I meant to do here, in this city so far removed from everything and everyone I knew? The answers eluded me, slipping through my fingers and leaving me feeling adrift and uncertain. I didn't know what I really had in store for me.

But within the ambiguity, there was a voice. It was soft and gentle, and it whispered words of encouragement and reassurance. It was as if God Himself was speaking to me, telling me to be patient and to trust in His plan, even when I couldn't see the way forward. And so, I clung to those words. I held on to the hope that there was a purpose to my presence in the Pacific Northwest, even if I couldn't yet see it. Thus, I waited with bated breath and an open heart. I trust that in due time, everything will be revealed.

Meanwhile, there were a lot of things to deal with. In a bid to sustain our company's viability, I was trying to do anything in my capacity. One such opportunity arose when I connected with a group in California. Recognizing the potential benefits of collaboration, I went to Monterey County, California, where negotiations with this group were to be carried out. We looked at our potential synergies and discussed the possibility of mutual assistance in which we both can be of help to each other. Traveling to Monterey County, California, I engaged in conversations with this group. And that is when we explored the prospect of merging our operations.

Initially, I felt optimistic about the collaboration and believed we could make it work. However, at the eleventh hour, our plans fell through, and the merger was off the table. We just decided to keep our company as it was and move forward. While the outcome was disappointing, it prompted a reevaluation of our strategic direction. It just wasn't meant to be. In retrospect, the failure of the merger presented unexpected advantages. When I returned to California, some details on the prospective partner's operations that had remained obscured during initial discussions also came to be known. These revelations emphasized the potential risks associated with merging our companies and depicted how we made the right decision.

After the incident, it seemed like I had left the place. However, the truth is I didn't resign from the company. I stayed with it, although I wasn't as actively involved after we lost that big contract. There were still opportunities and potential contracts down the line that kept us hopeful, but I don't want to jump ahead.

So, no, I never truly resigned from Olympus Consulting Group. I stayed on, trying to keep things going. It wasn't until later, when I moved to Pittsburgh, that I officially left. But that's for future chapters. The important thing is that I didn't give up on the company at that point. I stayed and did my best to ensure we remained successful.

During this time, I felt incredibly lost. My sense of purpose was blurred, so I didn't know what I was supposed to be doing. Drinking became a way to cope with this vagueness. Being in a new place where I had never been before only added to my disorientation. In spite of the beauty of the area, especially Seattle, which is truly a spectacular city, I felt out of place.

I lived closer to Tacoma, about 35 miles from downtown Seattle. The geological exquisiteness of the Pacific Northwest is undeniable. It's a magnificent part of the U.S. I often found myself wandering the streets, trying to soak in the ambiance and distract myself from my worries. But even in such a stunning environment, I struggled with feelings of purposelessness. I couldn't shake the feeling of being lost, and it was a tough period for me. It was as if I was searching for something that remained just out of reach.

***

At this time, both Bryan and I came up with an idea for a TV show called "Pots Unknown." We were inspired by Anthony Bourdain, the famous chef who took his own life. His show, "Parts Unknown," was aired on CNN, and he traveled to various interesting places around the world. Our concept was similar but focused on the cannabis industry. The idea was to travel around and visit different establishments that cultivated the cannabis plant, giving viewers an inside look at the industry. And because it was about cannabis, so the wordplay was at the words "Pots" and "Parts."

The show aimed to feature various companies involved in the cannabis business and represent their processes and unique approaches. Bryan and I were both really excited about this concept. We believed it had great potential and could attract a lot of interest. We envisioned ourselves traveling to different locations, interviewing people, and showcasing the diverse world of cannabis cultivation.

We pitched the idea to a production company, confident that they would see its potential. However, the feedback we received was that the name "Pots Unknown" was too similar to Anthony Bourdain's original "Parts Unknown." even though Anthony

Bourdain had passed away, the production company felt that the name was too close and they weren't interested in pursuing the project. This was a setback for us, but we didn't give up on the idea immediately.

We floated the concept around to other potential partners and even secured the website and domain name for "Pots Unknown." We were hopeful that someone would see the value in our idea and help bring it to life. Unfortunately, despite our efforts, the idea wasn't picked up by any production companies. It was disappointing because we believed in the concept and thought it could be successful.

Even though the show didn't materialize, the process of developing the idea was exciting and invigorating. It gave us a creative outlet and something to look forward to during a tough time. We poured a lot of energy into the project, and it was a learning experience for both of us. We gained insight into the production process and the challenges of getting a new show off the ground.

The idea of "Pots Unknown" somehow still remains in the back of my mind. I believe it was a ground-breaking concept that could have provided treasured awareness of the cannabis industry. The project allowed us to think outside the box and explore new possibilities, even if it didn't come to fruition. Now, I realize how important it is to keep pushing forward, even when things don't go as planned.

In the end, "Pots Unknown" remained an idea that could be revisited somewhere in the line. The cannabis industry is still growing and evolving, and there's always a chance that the concept could find its way to the right platform. For now, it serves as an endearing memory. And again, I found myself questioning what God had in store for me up here. I felt like I wasn't fulfilling my potential, but I wasn't sure what more I needed to do. I kept asking, *"What more is there? What should I be doing?"* It was a frustrating and confusing time. I wanted to feel like I was contributing more and that I had a clear objective. The query was gnawing at me. It was making me uneasy.

Then, an opportunity arose that seemed like it could change everything. We were approached to work for a large grocery chain. This wasn't just any grocery chain. It was one of the biggest on the West Coast. They wanted us to conduct threat assessments at all their distribution centers. These centers were scattered all over the West Coast, from California to Washington, and the contract would have been a significant boost for us. It felt like the break we desperately needed.

We put everything we had into preparing our pitch. We knew how important this was and how much was riding on it. When the day came, we headed to their regional office. Ready with data, presentations, and a strong sense of determination, we entered. The presentation went exceptionally well. They were impressed with our capabilities and what we could offer. There was intense excitement and relief. It felt like everything was finally falling into place. That all the hard work and the struggles were about to pay off.

However, just as we were on the brink of securing this major contract, COVID-19 hit. The quarantine measures came into effect, and everything shut down. This opportunity that seemed so promising was suddenly in jeopardy. However, this wasn't immediate. Before this situation, we were celebrating our successful pitch that weekend. We had flown in a colleague from Ohio to help with the presentation. After the pitch, which went incredibly well, we decided to celebrate. It was a fun weekend. We felt like we were on the verge of something big, something that could turn everything around for us.

However, by Sunday morning, reality set in. I had to take our colleague back to the airport, but I was still hungover from the night before. We had stayed up until about four o'clock in the morning, riding the high of what we thought was a major win for our company. The celebration had been a way to blow off steam and enjoy the moment.

My head was spinning in that morning's drive to the airport as I steered through the early morning traffic. Thus, I was still pretty hungover when I took him to the airport. When I dropped our colleague off at the airport, we exchanged our goodbyes. After dropping him off, I decided to stop by a couple of bars on the way back. That evening, on March 1st, things took a turn for the worse when I got pulled over by the police.

As I was driving, a young kid in a white vehicle came up on my right side. We were approaching a bridge. Well, what we could say was something like a bridge, and the right lane was coned off for construction. The kid whipped around me on the right, then abruptly swung into the left lane and hit the brakes. I had no time to react, and I ended up rear-ending their car. However, it wasn't a hard hit, as no airbags were deployed. Still, there was damage to both vehicles. That's when the police pulled me over. Getting handcuffed was a humiliating experience. I pride myself on being a professional driver. I was a driving instructor in Europe, training people to handle cars, buses, and military transport vehicles like deuce-and-a-halfs. I had driven in motorcades for dignitaries, serving as both the lead and backup driver. My driving skills were a point of honor for me. To find myself in a situation where I had hit someone, especially young kids, was devastating.

The driver of the other vehicle was only 19, probably still a relatively new driver. Irrespective of the circumstances leading up to the collision, the fact remained that I hit them from behind. In any rear-end collision, the driver who hits the other vehicle is typically at fault, no matter the situation. This knowledge added to my disappointment and frustration with myself.

As I sat there, handcuffed, I couldn't stop replaying the events in my mind. I had always considered myself a responsible and skilled driver, and yet here I was in a situation that contradicted that belief. It was a bitter pill to swallow, knowing that my actions had led to this outcome. My impression of professionalism and integrity in my driving abilities felt shattered.

The police took down the necessary information, and I was left to deal with the consequences of my actions. The incident served as a harsh memory that no matter how skilled or experienced one might be, a moment of poor judgment or bad luck can lead to repercussions. Especially the cons of drinking and driving were quite evident in the situation. The experience was sobering in more ways than one. It forced me to confront the reality of my state. I can't help but feel a deep sense of regret. The evening that had begun with the sweet moments with friends ended with me contemplating the need for change. The whole incident shook me to my core. Dr. Katherine Martin, also known as Dr. Katherine Fath, came and bailed me out. I was in jail for about two hours, but it felt like an eternity. Those two hours were more than enough to make me realize the gravity of my situation. When she bailed me out, she gave me a stern lecture about my responsibilities.

She was absolutely right to do so. Katherine is like my baby sister, even though she's Bryan's wife. I have always cared deeply for both Bryan and her. Her words touched me because I knew I should have been more responsible. She was justified in giving me a hard time, and I needed to hear it.

That night, I made a bold declaration to her. I told her I was never going to drink again. She looked at me, somewhat skeptical, and laughed a bit. She knew my patterns and probably thought it was an overreaction. But then, she shared some valuable insight with me. As an oncologist and a medical doctor, she told me, "Sy, if you're serious about quitting drinking, your skin color is going to change. You're going to look different."

She explained that I looked flushed, gray, and ashen every morning after drinking vodka, which was wreaking havoc on my system. Her words carried medical expertise and personal care. She said, "Your whole health outlook is going to change. Your skin will clear up, you'll look much better, and you'll feel much better."

She was absolutely right. Her advice and the seriousness of the situation made me realize the importance of her words. When she came to bail me out, she appeared like an angel. I was incredibly thankful for her help. They probably thought I was going to be stuck in jail for a while, with no one to bail me out.

But she did, and I will always be grateful for that. I hold Katherine and Bryan in the highest regard. They are as close to me as my own blood relatives. That night was a turning point in my life. I stopped drinking, and I have never looked back since then.

Seeing her waiting for me outside the jail was a profound relief. Her presence meant everything to me at that moment. It was clear that she and Bryan genuinely cared for my well-being. Their support and the harsh reality of my situation made me realize I needed to make a serious change. The words she spoke about my health were not just medical advice. They were a wakeup call.

The decision to stop drinking was not easy. But with Katherine's confidence, I found the strength to stick to it. As I embraced sobriety, I turned to my mom's Bible and started reading it that very night. It felt like a profound shift occurred within me. At that time, not everyone around me understood the significance of my calling because I myself wasn't fully aware of it. The changes I was undergoing were something nobody, including me, was prepared for.

Due to the DUI incident, I had to undergo a drug and alcohol evaluation. During my first session with one of the counselors, I felt an overwhelming urge to open up about my past suicide attempt. It was the first time I had ever spoken about it. The moment I blurted it out was incredibly emotional, and I believe it deeply moved the counselor. He listened intently, and after assessing my intake and responses, he told me that they didn't think I was an alcoholic. However, irrespective of his assessment, I insisted that I was. The act of sharing my darkest secrets seemed to have warmed the counselor greatly. I didn't understand what prompted me to reveal such a personal and painful part of my past, but I felt a divine intervention. It was as if God was urging me to start talking about it. I began to realize that the incident from 2015, which I had buried deep inside, needed to be addressed.

God seemed to communicate to me that the event in my office back in 2015 wasn't something to be hidden away. He confirmed to me that it was indeed Him present in that moment. For the longest time, I had kept that day locked away, hoping never to revisit it or discuss it. But now, it felt like God was coaxing me to bring it to the surface and confront it.

After this consciousness, my life was completely changed. I started to write about my experiences and began to talk about them openly. There was a new courage within me to come clean and discuss what had happened. This alteration allowed me to finally confront and process the trauma of that day in Denver on April 18th, 2015.

Reading my mom's Bible became a daily practice. The words brought me comfort and clarity. Each passage I read felt like a message that was delivered just for me. I began to understand the depth of my calling. I could see the route I needed to follow. The more I read, the more I felt a connection to something greater than myself. This spiritual voyage was an integral part of my recovery.

The sessions with the counselor continued, and each time, I found it easier to talk about my past. The counselor's empathy and understanding provided a safe space for me to unload the burdens I had been carrying. Sharing my story became therapy, helping me to heal from within. Talking about my suicide attempt was like a dam had burst. And with it, it had released all the repressed emotions that had been holding me back. I began to see the importance of confronting my demons directly instead of burying them. This openness brought a liberation that I had never experienced before.

The DUI incident, though a low point, forced me to seek help and face my issues. I am indebted to the intervention of both God and the counselor. God helped me to see the light in the darkest of times, and the counselor became my source.

During that transformative period in March, I experienced a series of premonitions, but one stood out vividly. It occurred during a trip to South Africa for a significant philanthropic endeavor. On Sundays, our group had the opportunity to attend church services, and the diversity of denominations among our members was striking. While some were Baptist and others Catholic, I identified as Presbyterian and attended services with fellow Presbyterian members.

***

During that period in March, I was having all these premonitions. Something remarkable happened at one particular service at a large Presbyterian church in Johannesburg, South Africa. We were traveling on Sundays, and the members were with us. They went to worship and perform church services.

There were a lot of members from different practices. Some of them were Baptist, some were Catholic, and I was Presbyterian. So, I would go to a Presbyterian service with other members of that church. It was shortly after the U.S. had initiated war with Iraq. This was somewhere around 2002 or 2003. As I listened to the minister delivering the sermon, I had a thoughtful realization. It was me standing at the pulpit, delivering the sermon. This dream felt incredibly real and impactful, leaving me drenched in sweat upon waking. The potency of the experience remained long after. It stirred an awe within me.

That dream seemed almost prophetic and prolific. Years later, I found myself regularly preaching at various churches. It was as though the dream had foretold my future had I remained committed to the course that God intended for me. He guided me toward sobriety and righteous living. It leads me to walk in obedience to His will. The beautiful dream was as though I had glimpsed into the imminent where my purpose was fulfilled.

During this time of growth and transformation, I began to dig into the Bible more earnestly than ever before. While I had owned a Bible for some time, I had not truly engaged with its teachings until then. It was as if God had finally captured my attention, leading me to dive into His word with fresh fervor. Looking back, I imagine God must have been amused by my devotion.

After years of spiritual exploration, it seemed I had finally found the path He had set before me. Well, if you ask, I'm sure God was really laughing. He had to be laughing, or at least that is how it sounds in my head. He must be saying that I finally got a hold of this guy after all these years. This is how I think it is. I believe God was pretty pleased with my progress.

# Chapter 14: Faith and Friendship

I was now intrigued by God's divine energies. Thus, I decided to enroll myself in some Seminary and Chaplaincy courses. However, I didn't have the means to attend a prestigious seminary or theological school. So, online courses were my only option. My financial circumstances were not very pleasing, and I could not afford any such traditional schools. You can only have an idea about my situation by knowing that I was living with friends. Irrespective of the limitations, I chose not to procrastinate my decision and give it my all. I was committing myself entirely to my studies. The quarantine period provided the perfect opportunity to focus. I was constantly absorbed in my studies and coursework for twelve to fourteen hours daily. I wanted to earn my credentials and become a chaplain.

No one could have guessed by my dedication that I was in just some online program. I didn't care if they were online. I wanted to make an impact, so I approached them with the same enthusiasm I would have given to any program in physical or offline settings. For others, it might just be about a random course, but for me, obtaining my credentials was not something I could take lightly. I desired them so badly that I did not let my lack of funds hinder it. On the contrary, it worked pretty well for me.

My decision was so quick that I think even God did not speculate on it. In fact, I felt as if God might have been pleasantly surprised by my decision to enroll. Of course, I say this with a touch of humor, and it should not be mistaken for blasphemy. I knew that God was aware of all my actions. However, it seemed as though my decision caught everyone off guard. I was the kind of person who often took people by surprise. And when I chose this route to ministry, the case was not much different. Some of my friends and family members had recognized that I was heading in this direction. Yet, many were taken aback and did not expect any such behavior on my part. Honestly, I was likely of such an abrupt change as it was in line with my character. I was the kind of person who loved to astonish people. In the same way, my decision to turn into ministry wasn't something people anticipated. Therefore, it became the most memorable part of my life and proved to be life-altering.

During this time, my dear friend Stacy Lollis helped me. I met Stacy when she was waiting tables at a place called the Ram Restaurant and Brewery. It was a brew house and restaurant where I often went to drink. I visited the place with my friend. I was struck by her beauty the moment I saw her. She was absolutely stunning! The image stayed with me, but her appeal goes far beyond her physical appearance. What drew me to her was her spirit and inner beauty, which radiated with an irresistible charm.

However, we didn't get to know each other during this initial meeting. We became acquaintances but were unaware of each other's true personalities. It was not until the quarantine hit that we became closer.

Before the pandemic, we were both training at the same gym. It was when the gyms shut down that we truly connected. My buddy Bryan, who I lived with in Washington, had built a gym in his garage. I jokingly referred to it as Bryan's Ark. It was an allusion to Noah from the Bible because of his zeal to create this reservation. When all the gyms closed due to the pandemic, we started working out in his garage, and it was during these sessions that Stacy began to join us. This was the turning point where we really bonded, as we spent more time together, and she began to open up to me, sharing her own life story.

Stacy has a story of her own, rich with experiences. Her life is filled with unique events and challenges, which is something she has shared with me extensively. Through these exchanges, I developed deep feelings for her. I genuinely love her, and she knows this, but we are just friends. This dynamic has been an important growth point for me.

Typically, I would've hit on her. However, with Stacy, I understand our purpose in each other's lives. This understanding has allowed our friendship to flourish. It's a special bond where she is my friend first and foremost, and I respect the boundaries and roles we play in each other's lives. This has been a friendship of maturity for me, where I recognized the value of a platonic relationship with someone I care deeply about.

Our relationship remains unique and deeply special. Our connection remains strong even though we don't meet as often as we used to. The place she has in my heart is only reserved for her. It is irreplaceable.

While my family is immensely important to me, Stacy is the one friend I feel completely comfortable sharing everything with. In the past, I was reserved and often kept my feelings and emotions to myself. But with Stacy, I can express my most personal thoughts without hesitation. She provided a safe space for me to be vulnerable as she listened to me without judgment.

I opened my heart and poured my soul into her in ways I thought impossible. It changed me from within. So, the material started to get incredibly intense when I was taking my chaplaincy course. There was this one section in it that was about the process of grief and the idea of how to deal with loss. In this part of the course, we dealt with the five stages of grief, which are denial, anger, bargaining, depression, and finally, acceptance.

The course required that I engage with these concepts on a very personal level. The coursework forced me to revisit my own experiences with loss, particularly the passing of my dad and my father-in-law. This introspection made the learning process heavy and emotionally taxing.

The instructor emphasized that the nature of chaplaincy work is inherently difficult due to its close association with hospices and cancer treatment facilities, where saying goodbye to dying patients is a regular part of the job.

The instructor told me that chaplains must have what they call a "soul friend." This soul friend is someone who can provide support and someone you can confide in and lean on when the emotional burden becomes too great. This concept acknowledged that chaplains and ministers are human and susceptible to emotional struggles, even though their job requires strength.

As soon as the instructor mentioned the need for a soul friend, I immediately knew who mine was. Without a doubt, I turned to Stacy. Our relationship has always been exclusively supportive and understanding. As I mentioned earlier, I can tell her anything, and she is always there to listen without judgment. I serve the same role for her. As a regular at her restaurant, Stacy had frequently served me and had seen firsthand my drinking habits. She probably thought, "Wow, this guy can really drink," as I often indulged heavily. Even after seeing this less flattering side of me, Stacy didn't judge. Instead, she observed and took note of who I was during those times. This familiarity with my old habits makes her perspective on my sobriety even more personal. She witnessed my entire transformation from a heavy drinker to someone who gave up alcohol.

As a matter of fact, Stacy didn't just see my transformation. She actively supported it. When I decided to quit drinking, she was there to encourage me. Though I was married and divorced twice, I had never been able to communicate so openly with my former wives. For some reason, I always held things in. With Stacy, however, as I said, it was different. I felt free to share what was truly on my mind and in my heart. Her support was not something I had experienced before.

Stacy was genuinely upset when she found out I had been in a homeless shelter, especially since I didn't tell her until after I had left. I was ashamed and kept it a secret from most people, only letting my immediate family know. Her disappointment in my secrecy led me to be open and honest in our relationship. From that point on, I vowed never to hold back from her again. I understood the importance of sharing everything with her, no matter how ashamed I might feel. Stacy has had a ringside seat to my transformation, and watching me change right before her eyes has brought us even closer.

One moment that helped me turn to Jesus was when Stacy sent me several YouTube links to the videos of Pastor Michael Todd of Transformation Church in Tulsa, Oklahoma. My interest in spirituality was becoming strong, and most churches were shuttered due to the pandemic. It was a link to one of his sermons entitled "Crazy Faith." As soon as I heard this sermon, it greatly impacted me. I believe it was meant to be that I heard that sermon, although I don't actively follow him today. After listening to his message on St. Patrick's Day, March 17th, 2020, I gave my life to Christ. That YouTube link was more than just a video. It was the beginning of my spiritual voyage. It led me to think. To think about the life I was leading. To think about how I owe it to God.

St. Patrick's Day is a very important day for me, and I hold it close. As I was an alcoholic and St. Patrick's Day was always a big celebration in my life, I was involved in the holiday wholeheartedly. Even as an honorary Irishman for the day, I was always participating in all its activities. I genuinely looked forward to the festivities and the drinking every year. It was a time when I could indulge in my love for alcohol.

The fact that I chose St. Patrick's Day to surrender my life to Christ feels deeply prophetic. It seemed like a moment when God displayed His sense of humor, particularly with me. Transforming such a day of drinking and celebration into a moment of thoughtful spirituality was quite ironic. It's as if God wanted to show that He could reach me even in my favorite indulgence. This decision was a huge change in my life.

The "Crazy Faith sermon was about faith. It explained how faith can change people's lives and make them better. I was so touched by this message as I had never been in my life. It was one of those sermons where you feel that the speaker is talking specifically about your concerns and difficulties. Of course, I knew he wasn't literally talking to me, but the message was so touching and timely that it felt prophetic. It made me realize the importance of walking in faith and being open to the changes that faith can bring. That St. Patrick's Day, I knew that I was meant to be on this ministry journey. Michael Todd's sermon taught me how to walk in faith and obedience to God, which has since become my mission. I am incredibly thankful to Stacy for sharing that link with me. She had no idea how impactful it would be, but it turned everything around for me. This experience taught me to be patient and improve as a father, son, brother, ex-husband, and friend.

Patience is something I pray for daily. This is because it hasn't always come naturally to me. When I deal with bad drivers on the road, I can be impatient. I was always weak in this area of my life and was trying to work on it. Eventually, I did learn it.

Improving myself as an individual has been a priority. I try to be a better ex-husband, maintaining respect even after the marriage ends. I strive to be a better father for the sake of my children. I want to shower them with only my love. I also would like to be close to my granddaughter, Joiee, and make an impact on her life constructively.

Being a better brother to my sister, Rhonda is also important to me. Our relationship means a lot, and I want to be there for her in meaningful ways.

As a friend, I attempt to be sympathetic and loyal to everyone around me. Each day presents growth opportunities, and I'm committed to evolving into the best version of myself in all these parts. At this point, I want to say something to all the readers who have traveled with me through these pages. They know I am deeply grateful for those ministers, mentors, and figures who have been there. Starting with Pastor Carmen Cox Harwell, who saw potential in me when I first shared my struggles. Then, my cousin, Reverend Edward Alan Scott, who shared his experiences with me, supported me during my chaplaincy training.

My Family has also been a strong provision in my life. My father-in-law, a Presbyterian minister, always guided me and gave me the wisdom I needed for this path. Also, my aunt, Elizabeth Scott, and the grace of Archbishop Desmond Tutu are imperative in my teachings. Their influence, even after their passing, continues to inspire my ministry.

During times of quarantine and isolation, their teachings helped me a lot. Though unable to engage in traditional internships or placements, I was content with their virtual guidance. I am particularly grateful for the friendships forged during unexpected circumstances like quarantine. These relationships—like the one I have with Stacy, who saw my change and actively helped me through it—have been priceless.

# Chapter 15: Pitt Stop

I want to express my gratitude to Katherine and Bryan Fath for welcoming me into their family in the Pacific Northwest. Without their generosity, I would have faced homelessness long ago. Living with them also turned me into a huge dog lover, as they had six dogs when I moved in. I sincerely appreciate and love those dogs. It was a beautiful experience, and I want to start this chapter by thanking them for giving me a home.

Now, when I talk about the "Pitt Stop," I'm referring to the city of Pittsburgh, which was a quick stop for me. I lived there for about eight months before moving to California. I stayed in Pittsburgh to work on a documentary that, unfortunately, we never completed. The production crew included James McDonough, Eden Herbert, and Danny Hickton.

Danny Hickton is an attorney in Pittsburgh. He and I had previously worked together in Denver at Dixie Brands. He was from Pittsburgh as well. He belonged to an area that was close to my home area. Thus, we hit it off well, and I mentored him while he was at Dixie. Danny eventually left Denver, returned to Pittsburgh, and pursued a law degree.

After reading an article I wrote called "Out of the Storm," Danny suggested it could make a compelling documentary. This idea planted the seed for our project. Apart from Danny, there was James McDonough. He was a videographer and animator for Cisco Systems in Pittsburgh. He brought his short stories, movies, and animation expertise to the team. Then Eden Herbert was our excellent writer and storyteller for the documentary. I left the

Pacific Northwest and headed to Pittsburgh in September 2021 to jumpstart the documentary "Project Resurrection" and watch my son, Sy the Fourth, play what I thought would be his final year of collegiate football. We began filming the documentary in Pittsburgh. During these eight months, the key players were James McDonough as the Videographer/Producer, Eden Herbert as the Writer/Storyteller, and Attorney Danny Hickton as the Chief Advisor. We conducted interviews and filmed stand-up shots throughout Pittsburgh. However, we faced an obstacle. It was the lack of funding. Fundraising was never my strong suit. I've never been comfortable asking for money to support projects. Thus, I was not able to do it this time as well.

We planned to create a 90-minute documentary but only managed to complete about 20 percent due to financial constraints. It was an ambitious project. Our aim was to capture compelling stories and visuals. We filmed at several locations around Pittsburgh, and our efforts resulted in a one-minute trailer that summarized the essence of the documentary. We had envisioned filming in various places, including Denver, the Pacific Northwest, and my old hometown. Though they were all very honest with their work, they had worked for free since I had no money to pay them. Eventually, I decided it was unfair to ask them to continue working without compensation.

We filmed various scenes, including my son's football game, gym sessions, and a Veterans Day parade. Yet, without the necessary funds, we couldn't proceed with on-location shoots. The documentary remains on hold even today. I couldn't secure the money needed and didn't want to take advantage of the crew's goodwill. This chapter of my life in Pittsburgh was a brief but intense period. It was filled with dreams and challenges. Irrespective of the project's hiatus, the experience was enough to know that I needed to tell my story to the world.

My son, Sy, played college football at Wheeling University in West Virginia during my time in Pittsburgh. I initially thought it was his final year, but he ended up receiving an additional year of eligibility. By the time he got this extra year, I had already moved to California. Therefore, my stay in Pittsburgh served a dual purpose. One was supporting Sy in what I believed was his final season. And second, launching "Project Resurrection," our documentary.

While I was in Pittsburgh, I also had the privilege of working with my sister's best friend, Miss Tawana Gatewood. She introduced me to Diane Powell, who ran a nonprofit organization called Community and Family Builders. This organization provided youth mentors to Penn Hills High School, specifically in their New Directions Program. Penn Hills is a suburb of Pittsburgh. It was at this high school that I realized the impact I could have. By becoming a youth mentor, I could affect young people's lives.

Thomas Gilcrease was the head counselor at Penn Hills High School and the leader of the New Directions Program. His presence in my life became imperative, which I realized later. Thomas was a deacon at a local Baptist church and a doctoral candidate in psychology. He was a gifted and compassionate individual. We quickly bonded, and he gave Miss Gatewood and me the freedom to engage with the students. We got engrossed with the students on a wide range of topics. New Directions was an alternative program designed for students who would otherwise face suspension. Students attended school on Saturdays to participate in this program. If not, then they were to be suspended. Although they weren't thrilled about spending their Saturday mornings in school, they chose the program over suspension.

Miss Gatewood and I worked as youth mentors under the Community and Family Builders organization. It was dedicated to educating and empowering community residents in Pittsburgh. Their mission was to address chronic and debilitating issues within the community. Diane Powell led the organization, and I had the opportunity to work alongside Miss Gatewood. She had been a lifelong family friend. We were paired up to mentor the youth.

It was Miss Gatewood who encouraged me to share my personal story, including my past suicide attempt, with the students. Initially, I was hesitant. However, I eventually opened up to the students about my experiences. This disclosure had a deep effect on the students. They began to pay attention and engage with us more openly. Sharing my story broke down the barriers between us and created a space for the students to share their own struggles.

The New Directions Program became a platform for these young people to express their issues and seek guidance. While it required the students to come to school on Saturdays to complete their homework, it also provided them with mentorship and support from people like Miss Gatewood and me. Though they were initially reluctant, they were soon satiated with the mentorship they received. During our time at Penn Hills High School, we witnessed the impact of our work firsthand. The New Directions Program aimed to provide a positive alternative for these students. Miss Gatewood's suggestion to share my personal story was the best idea. It opened up a new level of connection with the students. They began to trust us. They saw us as mentors who genuinely cared about their well-being. The floodgates opened, and students started sharing their own stories and struggles. It became clear that many of them were dealing with major issues. Our mentorship provided them with a safe space to talk about their problems.

They had lost a handful of students, young people who had just begun to steer through their lives. They were just trying to figure out what was going on. In a hand-to-hand struggle with the harsh realities of gun violence and other urban encounters, Tawana Gatewood and I arrived as youth mentors, and the students really opened up to us. They became so close to us that it drew them to share their own stories.

One particular incident stands out. After I shared my personal story, a young lady in the classroom revealed the scars on her arm from self-harm. This moment was a wake-up call for me. It made me realize the deep relevance and impact my story could have on others, especially the younger generation. My disclosure about my own suicide attempt seemed to unlock something in them.

It was an extremely moving experience. When you open your mind and heart, others often feel safe to do the same. If you're willing to open up your mind, people can identify with it. The young woman who showed me her scars asked me how I managed to overcome the mental struggles I faced. She said to me, "Mr. Sy," that's what the students called me, "How did you get over, you know, the mental part of it? How did you get over it?" I explained that writing had been my salvation and shared my article "Out of the Storm." She read it and felt as if I was speaking directly to her. She was like, "It almost felt like you were talking about me." This is the core message of my book. Although it is my personal story, its themes and lessons are universal. It speaks to anyone willing to confront their issues. It is regardless of age or any other factors. It's my story, but it can apply to anybody. You can be elderly or a young kid. It doesn't matter if you're willing to open up and acknowledge if you have problems. I'm writing not only about myself but also about other people who are suffering.

This young woman's courage left a lasting impression on me. After I moved to California, Miss Gatewood told me that the girl had stood up in front of her class to share her own story. Ms. Tawana Gatewood said, "Sy, you would have been so proud of her.

She got up in front of the class and read her own story. And she was able to articulate that to the rest of the kids." I was immensely proud of her bravery. Given that she was only 16 at the time, I sought her parents' permission to speak with her. And I told her, "That's a beautiful thing that you're willing to get up and talk to your peers about things that you have gone through." Her willingness to open up to her peers about her struggles is my victory.

Thus, my story resonates with many because it is not just about my experiences. It also addresses the struggles of others who suffer in silence. As a chaplain working with cancer patients, I had become accustomed to dealing with pain and suffering.

However, as a mentor in a high school, particularly with students who had been suffering, I presented a new perspective on my experiences. These young people had been closed off for so long that their ability to communicate had been severely impacted.

They were just coming off the pandemic, so it was a very emotional time for them. I'm glad I was able to share my story with them because it changed the way they communicated with Miss Gatewood and me.

So, I stayed there for about eight months. I was staying with my sister, Rhonda Elaine Alli, and her husband, Rick James. They provided me with a place to stay while in Pittsburgh. My sister is truly my "Ride or Die" partner and the most faithful sister a brother can have. I will always be grateful for everything she did for me.

I also had a chance to spend some quality time with Sy the Fourth, my son. And even though I was in Pittsburgh, I was still working with one of the cancer patients from the Pacific Northwest. So, I was still working with young people, and I was working with some of the cancer patients. It was an interesting situation but also very fulfilling.

Nevertheless, I just knew that I wasn't going to be in Pittsburgh for a long period of time. Without a clue about where I was headed, I decided to move. I have always loved California since I lived there in the early nineties. I knew it was expensive, but I always knew I might end up back in California at some point. Granting that my son ended up and got another year of eligibility due to the pandemic, I knew Pittsburgh was not my final destination. However, I was unsure of where life was taking me after Pittsburgh. I'm still not sure why I left Pittsburgh and went to California, but it was God guiding me there for reasons I would eventually find out. At the time, I could only think that Pittsburgh was not where I belonged. In April of 2022, I left and went to California. Nonetheless, in that time in Pittsburgh, I began to realize that I had this connection with young people.

There was a bond between me and these high school kids even though I was old enough to be not only their parent but maybe their grandparents.

Hence, as I said, I knew I wasn't going to stay in Pittsburgh. Yet, I felt my heart heavy. I had to leave those kids because we were just getting to a point where they were opening up and telling some deep-rooted details.

These emotions they shared that were going on in their hearts and minds were so essential for them to move on with their lives and live them to the fullest. Thus, leaving them was not easy. It was a pivotal moment. That's the reason I call it a pit stop. It is just a play on the word Pittsburgh because it was pretty brief, but that's where I got the idea that I can work with young people, no matter how old or how young they are. I can work with pretty much anybody and everybody.

It was an affirmation that I definitely have something to give to young people, particularly if they're struggling with mental health. That's my platform. I didn't know what I was going to be running into when I came to California. All I could say is that Pittsburgh was very fascinating, and it was always good to be home. Even though I grew up north of Pittsburgh, I always considered it my adopted home.

# Chapter 16: California Dreaming

I came out to California in April of 2022 to work for a security company. They recruited me to come out as their executive director. I didn't know how that would work. I knew it was a very small company. I was only there for a couple of months. So, it didn't work out.

The thing that happened there is, number one, they didn't have funds to put me up in housing. So I lived in my office for two months, from April until June. I didn't really have a suitable place to live. The company came to me on a Sunday in June and told me they were shutting down operations. They said if I wanted to return to Pittsburgh or the Pacific Northwest, they would give me a plane ticket. I denied it. I said I'm going to stay in California. They were very curious and couldn't understand why I wanted to stay. This was because I had no friends or family in the area.

Despite having no place to live and, at that point, no job, I felt compelled to stay. They took back the company car they had given me, so I literally had nothing. However, I had enough money in my pocket to stay at a Best Western hotel in Marina, California. It was right on the beach, and I stayed there for one night. That night was the first time I had actually slept in a comfortable bed after two months.

This was because I had been sleeping on a pullout couch in my office during that time. The company didn't have the money to put me up as they had promised. Instead of placing me in a hotel for a couple of weeks, they bought me a futon, a couch that pulls out into a bed. I slept there, but it wasn't the best situation.

According to the government, I was homeless because the office wasn't a place that provided housing. It was a small office, so I was considered homeless. I made it official when I ended up going to the Veterans Transition Center. Now, I was officially homeless. The Veterans Transition Center, or VTC, was located at the old Fort Ord Army Base in California. It was basically a homeless shelter for veterans. I got up the next morning and took an Uber to the Veterans Transition Center.

That was how I really got started in California because the security company didn't work out. I later found out that the company hadn't really closed down. It was a ploy to get me to leave. I never understood why they didn't just come to me and say that they didn't have the money. And that it wasn't going to work out. It would have been more honorable to just tell me the truth. Instead, they told me they were closing the company down when they did not.

A few months into my stay in California, I had to go to the VA hospital in Palo Alto. It was north of where I was living. That is when I found out that the company was still open. It was unnecessary for them to lie. I have nothing against them. But I would have appreciated it if they were honest with me. They could have simply said, "We don't have the money. We don't think this is going to work out." We could have parted ways honorably. Yet, they weren't upfront, which was disappointing.

However, I do not care about their deceit. It didn't matter in the grand scheme of things because God had other plans for me. Their actions, though potentially hurtful, actually did me a huge favor. The old Fort Ord Army Base, where the VTC was located, had been shut down in 1994 under the base realignment and closure authorized by President Clinton. The base was huge, almost the size of two cities, but they still had some housing areas where they housed homeless veterans. At the VTC, I had four or five housemates with whom I shared the space in Marina, California. I got to know my housemates once I got situated and got my bearings. I realized that this was a very important step for me. I reconciled with my housemates. The support we offered each other was invaluable. This period of my life was unexpected and initially unwanted. However, it did become most dear to me.

I now understand what it's like to be homeless. I know what it feels like to be without money and not have a job. I went through all of that. This experience gave me a deeper empathy and understanding. It developed an emotion for those without stable housing. The security company's dishonesty led me to a place where I could make a real difference in people's lives.

I felt dismayed and confused when I arrived at the VTC. I thought perhaps God was upset with me. Here I was! Having been successful in my line of work. Suddenly, I found myself in a homeless shelter. With no money, no car, and no job! I thought it was the end for me. It turned out that it was just the beginning.

I asked God why He had put me in this situation. His response was clear. He asked me, "You're a chaplain, right?" I answered, "Yes." He then guided me to embrace my role and use my skills to help the other veterans around me. He pointed out that there were many veterans who could benefit from my guidance and support. I took His advice and began to minister to the veterans at the VTC. Once I started engaging with the other veterans, I realized that many of them were facing much greater challenges than I was. They struggled with PTSD, mental health issues, and alcohol problems. My situation was although difficult. However, it paled in comparison to what they were enduring. It became clear that my presence at the VTC was a godsend. It was not just for me. It was for the veterans I was able to help. This experience taught me that sometimes life halts our footsteps only to give momentum in the future. It is actually a step towards fulfilling a greater purpose.

***

I didn't have any money, so to get state funds, I received $300 a month from California. This small amount helped cover my phone bill and a few other essentials. To earn this money, I had to work at a public works department in Del Rey Oaks, California. The head of public works gave us work assignments, and I was tasked with cleaning the bathrooms at a local park. It wasn't glamorous, but I took the initiative and worked very hard.

The director of public works noticed my dedication and my physique. I told him that I was a chaplain. I also informed him about my condition at the homeless shelter. He decided to give me some of the workers with issues like PTSD. He thought I might be able to help them out.

So, while I was cleaning toilets and picking up garbage, I was also helping other people. The director took a liking to me. In short, we hit it off well. Even though I was only making $300 a month, I worked diligently. The director noticed this. He told me he didn't think I'd be homeless for long. He believed God had something spectacular in store for me. At the time, I laughed about it. I thought, "We'll see." However, things indeed got better. I noticed an Anytime Fitness Center across the street while staying at the shelter. Anytime Fitness is a big chain of fitness centers. I didn't have any money to join it at the time. Anyway, I went in and met the owner. I explained that I was staying across the street. They could see that I worked out and was fit. The general manager of Anytime Fitness came up with a generous plan, allowing me to use the gym for free for two or three months until I could afford to pay. God was truly placing the right people in my path, and I was incredibly thankful to the manager for giving me a place to work out.

I found my new church, His Grace Ministries, through RJ, a retired Army Ranger who had served multiple tours in Afghanistan and Iraq. Now, he struggled with PTSD and was going through a lot, but we managed to bond and share our experiences. He worked as a chef at a local Greek restaurant and often brought gyros home for me. Late at night, we would sit and talk, sharing our stories. One evening, he mentioned a church service held every Sunday at the VTC, which I hadn't been aware of.

RJ took me to the service one Sunday, where I met the congregation from His Grace Ministries International, led by Pastor Enrique Cardenas. Pastor Enrique and I quickly connected, and I started attending church regularly. I grew to love the church and the community. However, due to some issues, the church had to move from the VTC back to Salinas, California, and services were held at Pastor Enrique's house. Despite the change, I remained committed to His Grace Ministries. Finding my church home was a blessing. The spiritual aspect of my life began to reform as I connected with the church and its members. I took my housemates to church services, and things developed positively for me at His Grace Ministries. I became an usher and grew more involved over time. At our monthly men's breakfasts, I shared my testimony about my suicide attempt, which seemed to empower me. The men were drawn to my story and wanted to hear more about my background. Things were starting to take shape, and I felt better about my situation, even though I was still in a shelter.

At the Veterans Transition Center, my case manager, Charlie Schmidt, was adamant that I get an office to use for my chaplaincy. This office allowed me to counsel some of the guys dealing with PTSD, alcoholism, drug abuse, and other issues. Having this space was a significant step forward, and things were starting to improve. It was a slow process. But progress was being made.

I became more involved in helping others with each passing day. I was helping both at the shelter and in the broader community. The public works department provided me with much-needed funds and allowed me to connect with people who needed my support. This work and my growing role at the church gave me a renewed sense of purpose and direction.

The director of public works continued to be a source of encouragement, reminding me that my hard work and dedication were not going unnoticed. His belief in my potential helped sustain me during the toughest times. Similarly, the generosity of the Anytime Fitness manager provided a physical outlet that was essential for my well-being. These acts of kindness and support from the community were crucial in helping me rebuild my life.

My housemate at the VTC, Brad Burns, was an 80-year-old man with a car, but he couldn't drive due to past driving infractions. So, I began driving him around, which gave me access to his vehicle. When I started applying for jobs, I found a position as a youth mentor in a local school district.

I told Brad about the job and mentioned needing a car for the interview. Generously, Brad offered me his car to use. He said, "

Well, I can't drive my car. You've been driving me around. So why don't you just take the car to go to the job interview?" So, I did.

I interviewed with a company. It was called Elevo, which focused on coaching, and I got hired as a youth coach. This job was a blessing in disguise, and Brad's support was helpful for my mental and financial growth. I desperately needed the job, as I had no money at all. The job with Elevo allowed me to commute to that school.

In January 2023, I was promoted to management, which improved my financial situation. By April, however, my time at the VTC had run out, and I had to leave. Without a permanent place to stay, I began renting Airbnb in Salinas and Pacific Grove, California.

# Chapter 17: Coach Sy

When I first started as a youth coach, I was assigned to TK1st grade, which includes transitional kindergarten, kindergarten, and 1st graders. These are really young kids—a massive change from when I was in Pittsburgh, where I worked with high school students. So, I went from high school kids to essentially just babies.

Basically, we're talking about first grade. Therefore, I needed to find a way to ensure the kids understood what we were trying to accomplish with Elevo. The children know me as Coach Sy, and I had to navigate the fine line between being Reverend Sy and Coach Sy. I had to ensure that the separation between church and state was respected and never crossed. In school, when interacting with these kids as Coach Sy, I had to act as a mentor rather than a chaplain to avoid conflicts with the church and state doctrines prohibiting bringing religion into schools.

Irrespective of the current political discussions suggesting that religion might become more present in schools, such as teaching the Ten Commandments, I had to be very careful. As Coach Sy, my role was to mentor, almost like ministering in schools, but without directly quoting Bible scriptures to the kids.

By doing this, I could still minister by being a mindful and good mentor. I hope this explanation makes sense, as it was crucial for me to avoid any situation where school administrators might tell me that, although they know I'm a chaplain, I cannot preach to the kids. It was a delicate balance, but I believe I managed it well. I could still mentor the kids effectively, and in a way, it felt like ministering. Therefore, the line between being a minister and a mentor in school was a bit blurred. However, I found that I was a good mentor, able to connect with the kids, even the young ones. To understand Elevo better, you need to know that it is an educational company. It offers a variety of inschool and out-of-school programs and services. It aims to support the physical and mental well-being of all students. This, in turn, helps them in their academics.

Among school programs, they provide in-school programs. These include lunch and recess programs. And then there are the after-school programs. These programs are designed to teach kids good sportsmanship and teamwork through various games. So, we organize sports events for them. Though these children were very young, which is quite different from my previous experience in Pittsburgh with high school students, the essence of Elevo's programs remains consistent.

When I moved to California, I had no idea that I would end up working in elementary schools as a youth coach and mentor, but my experience with older kids helped me adjust. I can't share personal experiences, like my own suicide attempt, with such young children because they wouldn't understand it.

However, I have a keen sense for recognizing when kids are struggling, a skill I believe is God-given. I work with very young coaches, some as young as my 23-year-old son, Sy. Often, I find myself mentoring both the coaches and the students. These young coaches, aged 19 to 22, frequently come to me when they encounter students with problems. I talk to the kids and often find out that their issues at home affect their school life. Many young coaches are not equipped to handle such situations, but my background as a chaplain and counselor for cancer patients and veterans with PTSD helps me connect with these children and earn their trust. This job has been a blessing, especially considering my past experiences, including time spent in a homeless shelter. Now, working full-time as a site success manager, I still see myself as a coach. The kids call me Coach Sy, and I insist they don't use my first name, nor do I let them call the other coaches by their first names. This formality helps establish respect for the young coaches, who, despite their age, are mentors.

Management understands and supports this approach, knowing it helps maintain the coaches' authority. The young coaches appreciate this structure, too, even if they laugh about how strict I am. This respect is crucial because it reinforces the mentor-student relationship. Working with these kids has been incredibly rewarding, and Elevo has been very supportive of my efforts to address mental health and provide meaningful assistance to the students.

Elevo's support has allowed me to use my skills to spot and help struggling kids. It's a wonderful feeling to identify issues and provide help because I've dealt with similar problems with older students before. Elevo is an ideal fit for me because I can mentor both the students and the young coaches, who are often close to my son's age. This role has allowed me to be a mentor to everyone in Elevo. Elevo brings various programs with Social Emotional Learning "SEL" based programs in school districts across California. It's a growing company within the state, providing support through physical education classes and other activities that promote social-emotional learning. After the pandemic and the extended quarantine period, we noticed many issues among students who had been isolated for a long time. When they returned to school, they struggled with re-adjusting to social environments. Elevo's programs have become more important than ever, helping kids in numerous aspects of their lives. The company's mission aligns perfectly with my passion for mentoring and mental health advocacy. We help students develop crucial life skills, provide emotional support, and encourage physical activity. Elevo's comprehensive approach to student wellbeing makes a significant difference, especially in the current post-pandemic context. The combination of my chaplaincy and coaching skills allows me to provide unique and effective support to both students and young coaches.

I continue to find joy in working with these children and supporting them through Elevo's programs. The respect and trust I receive from the kids and the coaches reinforce my commitment to this work. Elevo truly makes a difference. Working with them has allowed me to help these young students navigate their challenges. The company's growth and impact across California highlight the importance of our work and the positive changes we bring to students' lives.

Elevo is an educational company that truly makes a difference. Working with Elevo has allowed me to blend my skills and passions effectively. It made a lasting impact on the lives of young students and the young coaches who guide them. This harmonious relationship with Elevo continues to inspire and motivate me, reinforcing the value of the work we do every day.

***

As I mentioned in a previous chapter, my friend RJ introduced me to His Grace Ministries International. I've grown with them. Now, I'm part of the leadership team, heading the Usher and Greeter team on Sundays and co-leading our men's outreach ministry. We hold a Bible breakfast one Saturday a month.

Additionally, we minister to an Alcoholics Anonymous home in Salinas every Monday, where many men struggle with alcohol and drug abuse. My involvement has deepened with this ministry, and I preach on Sundays about once every three or four months. I also preach to our men regularly.

Being part of this ministry has been fantastic now that I'm in California. It feels like I have a true church home. This ministry is growing in Salinas, California. Pastor Enrique and his wife, Pastor Ileana, have entrusted me with many responsibilities, and I've risen to the occasion. Spiritually, I've grown even more since coming out here. Regardless of being a chaplain already, His Grace Ministries has me doing more outreach, especially bringing men into the fold of Christ. This experience has been incredible, and I've grown exponentially here.

I've evolved from being just a member to being part of the church's executive leadership team. I have a say in how we handle ushering, greeting our congregation in the morning, and other church program aspects. My growth parallels the church's growth. The pastors, our praise and worship team, and everything else are expanding. I'm very happy, honored, and humbled to be a part of the church's growth.

***

I want to share what inspired me to write this book as I reach the end. God inspired me. I had no desire to write this book. The last thing I wanted to expose, being a private person, was my own missteps and struggles. However, God made it clear to me that writing this book was necessary.

He told me that it would help not only me but also others who struggle with mental health issues in silence, those who battle depression or PTSD without admitting it. I was reluctant, but God reminded me of his guidance in my life. He said, "I came for you. Now, I need you to write about this."

I began writing and documenting as a form of therapy. It was a practice I encouraged young students at Penn Hills High School to do. Writing has been relaxing for me. And helping others through my writing has been even more fulfilling.

Thus, this book is not just about me. It is about reaching out to others who are struggling. I hope to bring others out of the dusk by putting my experiences on paper and sharing them. While some may respond negatively, calling me weak for not admitting my problems earlier, I know that many people with depression prefer to keep their struggles hidden. This book is meant to bring these issues into the open. It is to encourage people to seek help and talk about their mental health.

I love the metaphor of a lighthouse. I have always been drawn to lighthouses living near the Pacific Ocean. It guides ships in trouble back to safety. Similarly, there are many lost souls who need help and direction. Writing this book is my way of being a lighthouse, guiding those who are lost back to the shores of safety and light. My role in this is minor compared to the potential impact this book can have on others. It is designed to inspire people to seek help, talk about their mental health issues, and start writing about their experiences. This is how I measure the success of this book. I have some future plans. I have a manuscript titled "Corporate Smokejumper" that explores my career in the protection industry, the people I protected, and the situations I encountered.

While I only touched on this in the current book, which focuses more on faith and how it helps you navigate tough times, I still have plans to finish "Corporate Smokejumper." This future project will explore a different aspect of my life and experiences, but the underlying theme of overcoming challenges and seeking help will remain central.

Here's a personal note from me to the readers. You need to understand that there is light at the end of the tunnel. Many people are deeply depressed and stuck in darkness. This book is a lifeline that is meant to inspire and help those who are struggling.

This could be an emotional struggle or a mental struggle. It could even be physical or financial. I hope my experiences encourage others to seek help. If you can't reach out to me, reach out to a minister, a psychologist, or someone who can help you transition from darkness into light.

I was a professional at the top of my game as a security expert and advisor. Yet, I still suffered from massive depression. Professionals in any industry can struggle with mental health. Your professional or socio-economic status doesn't matter. You could be homeless or living in a mansion, and depression can affect you. I want people to know that help is available and that seeking it is imperative. If people see my journey and think, "Sy was a professional athlete, entertainer, university lecturer, and world traveler who protected people. Yet, he struggled and overcame it," maybe they'll see hope for themselves. That's the message I want to convey: there's always a way out. No matter where you are in life. Pursuing help is the first step.

www.ingramcontent.com/pod-product-compliance
Lightning Source LLC
Chambersburg PA
CBHW070832160726
48004CB00001B/342